PETER STUYVESANT,

THE

LAST DUTCH GOVERNOR OF NEW AMSTERDAM.

BY

JOHN S. C. ABBOTT,

ILLUSTRATED.

NEW YORK:
DODD & MEAD, No. 762 BROADWAY.
1873.

New Amsterdam.

PETER STUYVESANT,

THE

LAST DUTCH GOVERNOR

OF

NEW AMSTERDAM.

BY

JOHN S. C. ABBOTT.

ILLUSTRATED.

NEW YORK:
DODD & MEAD, No. 762 BROADWAY.
1875.

PREFACE.

IT is impossible to understand the very remarkable character and career of Peter Stuyvesant, the last, and by far the most illustrious, of the Dutch governors of New Amsterdam, without an acquaintance with the early history of the Dutch colonies upon the Hudson and the Delaware. The Antiquarian may desire to look more fully into the details of the early history of New York. But this brief, yet comprehensive narrative, will probably give most of the information upon that subject, which the busy, general reader can desire.

In this series of " *The Pioneers and Patriots of America*," the reader will find, in the " Life of De Soto," a minute description of the extreme south and its inhabitants, when the Mississippi rolled its flood through forests which the foot of the white man had never penetrated. " Daniel Boone " conducts us to the beautiful streams and hunting grounds of Kentucky, when the Indian was the sole possessor

of those sublime solitudes.   In the " Life of Miles
Standish, the Puritan Captain," we are made familiar
with that most wonderful of all modern stories, the
settlement of New England.   " Peter Stuyvesant "
leads us to the Hudson, from the time when its majestic waters were disturbed only by the arrowy
flight of the birch canoe, till European colonization
had laid there the foundations of one of the most
flourishing cities on this globe.

In these Histories the writer has spared no labor
in gathering all the information in his power, respecting those Olden Times, now passing so rapidly
into oblivion.

JOHN S. C. ABBOTT.

CONTENTS.

CHAPTER I.

Discovery of the Hudson River.

CHAPTER II.

The Progress of Discovery.

CHAPTER III.

The Commencement of Colonization.

PETER STUYVESANT.

CHAPTER I.

Discovery of the Hudson River.

The Discovery of America.—Colonies.—The Bay of New York.—
Description of the Bay.—Voyage of Sir Henry Hudson.—Dis-
covery of the Delaware.—The Natives.—The Boat Attacked.—
Ascending the Hudson.—Escape of the Prisoners.—The Chiefs
Intoxicated.— The Return.— The Village at Castleton.—The
Theft and its Punishment.—The Return to England.

ON the 12th of October, 1492, Christopher Co-
lumbus landed upon the shores of San Salvador, one
of the West India islands, and thus revealed to astonished Europe a new world. Four years after this,
in the year 1496, Sebastian Cabot discovered the
continent of North America. Thirty-three years
passed away of many wild adventures of European
voyagers, when, in the year 1539, Ferdinand de Soto
landed at Tampa Bay, in Florida, and penetrating
the interior of the vast continent, discovered the

Mississippi River. Twenty-six years more elapsed ere, in 1565, the first European colony was established at St. Augustine, in Florida.

In the year 1585, twenty years after the settlement of St. Augustine, Sir Walter Raleigh commenced his world-renowned colony upon the Roanoke. Twenty-two years passed when, in 1607, the London Company established the Virginia Colony upon the banks of the James river.

In the year 1524, a Florentine navigator by the name of Jean de Verrazano, under commission of the French monarch, Francis I., coasting northward along the shores of the continent, entered the bay of New York. In a letter to king Francis I., dated July 8th, 1524, he thus describes the Narrows and the Bay:

"After proceeding one hundred leagues, we found a very pleasant situation among some steep hills, through which a very large river, deep at its mouth, forced its way to the sea. From the sea to the estuary of the river, any ship heavily laden might pass, with the help of the tide, which rises eight feet. But as we were riding at anchor, in a good berth, we would not venture up in our vessel without a knowledge of the mouth. Therefore we took the boat, and entering the river, we found the country, on its banks, well peopled, the inhabitants not much differing from the others, being dressed out with the feathers of birds of various colors.

"They came towards us with evident delight, raising loud shouts of admiration, and showing us where we could most securely land with our boat. We passed up this river about half a league, when we found it formed a most beautiful lake three leagues in circuit, upon which they were rowing thirty or more of their small boats, from one shore to the other, filled with multitudes who came to see us. All of a sudden, as is wont to happen to navigators, a violent contrary wind blew in from the sea, and forced us to return to our ship, greatly regretting to leave this region which seemed so commodious and delightful, and which we supposed must also contain great riches, as the hills showed many indications of minerals."

In the year 1609, a band of Dutch merchants, called the East India Company, fitted out an expedition to discover a northeast passage to the Indies. They built a vessel of about eighty tons burden, called the Half Moon, and manning her with twenty sailors, entrusted the command to an Englishman, Henry Hudson. He sailed from the Texel, in his solitary vessel, upon this hazardous expedition, on the 6th of April, 1609. Doubling North Cape amid storms and fog and ice, after the rough voyage of a month, he became discouraged, and determined to change his plan and seek a northwest passage.

Crossing the Atlantic, which, in those high latitudes, seems ever to be swept by storms, he laid in a store of codfish on the banks of Newfoundland, and, on the 17th of July, ran his storm-shattered bark into what is now known as Penobscot Bay, on the coast of Maine. Here he found the natives friendly. He had lost his foremast in a storm, and remained at this place a week, preparing a new one. He had heard in Europe that there was probably a passage through the unexplored continent, to the Pacific ocean, south of Virginia. Continuing his voyage southward, he passed Cape Cod, which he supposed to be an island, and arrived on the 18th of August at the entrance of Chesapeake Bay. He then ran along the coast in a northerly direction and entered a great bay with rivers, which he named South River, but which has since received the name of the Delaware.

Still following the coast, he reached the Highlands of Neversink, on the 2d of September, and at three o'clock in the afternoon of the same day, came to what then seemed to him to be the mouths of three large rivers. These were undoubtedly the Raritan, the Narrows, and Rockaway Inlet. After careful soundings he, the next morning, passed Sandy

The "Half Moon."

Hook and anchored in the bay at but two cables' length from the shore. The waters around him were swarming with fish. The scenery appeared to him enchanting. Small Indian villages were clustered along the shores, and many birch canoes were seen gliding rapidly to and fro, indicating that the region was quite densely populated, and that the natives were greatly agitated if not alarmed by the strange arrival.

Soon several canoes approached the vessel, and the natives came on board, bringing with them green tobacco and corn, which they wished to exchange for knives and beads. Many vessels, engaged in fishing, had touched at several points on the Atlantic coast, and trafficked with the Indians. The inhabitants of this unexplored bay had heard of these adventurers, of the wonders which they brought from distant lands, and they were in a state of great excitement, in being visited in their turn.

The bay was fringed with the almost impenetrable forest. Here and there were picturesque openings, where Indian villages, in peaceful beauty, were clustered in the midst of the surrounding foliage. The natives were dressed in garments of deer skin, very softly tanned, hanging gracefully about their persons, and often beautifully ornamented. Many of them wore mantles of gorgeously-colored feathers, quite artistically woven together; and they had also garments of rich furs.

The following morning a party from the vessel landed, in a boat, on the Jersey shore. They were received with great hospitality by the natives, who led them into their wigwams, and regaled them with dried currants, which were quite palatable. As they had no interpreters, they could only communicate with each other by signs. They found the land generally covered with forest trees, with occasional meadows of green grass, profusely interspersed with flowers, which filled the air with fragrance.

Another party of five men, was sent to examine the northern shore of the bay. They probably inflicted some gross outrage upon the natives, as the crew of the Half Moon had conducted infamously, at other points of the coast, where they had landed, robbing and shooting the Indians. The sun had gone down, and a rainy evening had set in, when two canoes impelled rapidly by paddles, overtook the returning boat. One contained fourteen Indians; the other twelve. Approaching within arrow shot, they discharged a volley into the boat. One of these keen-pointed weapons, struck John Coleman in the throat, and instantly killed him. Two other Englishmen were wounded.

The Indians seemed satisfied with their revenge.

Though they numbered twenty-six warriors, and there were but two white men left unwounded, the savages permitted them to continue their passage to the vessel, without further molestation. The journalist, who records this assault, is silent respecting the provocation which led to it.

Hudson was alarmed by this hostility, and expected an immediate attack upon the ship. He promptly erected bulwarks along the sides of his vessel as a protection from the arrows of the fleet of war canoes, with which, he supposed, he would be surrounded the next morning.

But the night passed quietly away; the morning dawned, and a few canoes approached from another part of the bay, with no signs of hostility. These peaceful Indians had manifestly heard nothing of the disturbance of the night before. They came unarmed, with all friendly attestations, unsuspicious of danger, and brought corn and tobacco, which they offered in exchange for such trinkets as they could obtain. The next morning, two large canoes approached from the shores of the bay which was many leagues in extent, one of which canoes seemed to be filled with warriors, thoroughly armed. The other was a trading boat.

It is probable that those in the war canoe, came as a protection for their companions. It is hardly conceivable that the Indians, naturally timid and wary, could have thought, with a single war canoe containing scarcely a dozen men, armed with arrows, to attack the formidable vessel of Sir Henry Hudson, armed, as they well knew it to be, with the terrible energies of thunder and lightning.

The Indians were so unsuspicious of danger, that two of them unhesitatingly came on board. Sir Henry, we must think treacherously, seized them as prisoners, and ordered the canoes containing their companions, to keep at a distance. Soon another canoe came, from another direction, with only two men in it. Sir Henry received them both on board, and seized them also as prisoners. He intended to hold them as hostages, that he might thus protect himself from any hostility on the part of the natives.

One of these men upon finding himself a captive, leaped overboard and swam ashore. Sir Henry had now three prisoners and he guarded them very closely. Yet the natives, either from policy or from fear, made no hostile demonstrations against him.

The half Moon remained in the outer bay nine days. Several exploring tours had been sent out, visiting what is now known as the Jersey shore. None of these, with the exception of the one to which we have alluded, encountered any hostility whatever from the natives.

On the 11th of September, Hudson sailed through the Narrows, and anchored in the still and silent waters of New York harbor. These· waters had never then been whitened by a sail, or ploughed by any craft larger than the Indian's birch canoe. The next morning, the 12th of September, Sir Henry again spread his sails, and commenced his memorable voyage up the solitary river, which has subsequently borne his name. Only here and there could a few wigwams be seen, scattered through the forest, which fringed its banks. But human life was there, then as now, with the joys of the bridal and the grief of the burial. When we contemplate the million of people, now crowded around the mouth of the Hudson, convulsively struggling in all the stern conflicts of this tumultuous life, it may be doubted whether there were not as much real happiness in the wigwam of the Indian as is now to be found in the gorgeous palace of the modern millionaire. And when we contemplate the vices and the crimes which civilization has developed, it may also be doubted whether there were not as much virtue, comparatively with the numbers to be found, within the bark hut of the red man, as is now to be

found in the abodes of the more boastful white
man.

Sir Henry Hudson hoped to find this majestic
river, inviting him into unknown regions of the
north, to be an arm of the sea through which he
could cross the continent to the shores of the Pacific. It was not then known whether this continent were a few miles or thousands of miles in
breadth. For the first two days the wind was contrary, and the Half Moon ascended the river but
about two miles. The still friendly natives paddled
out from the shores, in their bark canoes, in great
numbers, coming on board entirely unarmed and
offering for sale, excellent oysters and vegetables in
great abundance.

On the third day a strong breeze sprang up from
the southeast. All sail was set upon the Half
Moon. It was a bright and beautiful autumnal day.
Through enchanting scenery the little vessel ploughed the waves of the unknown river, till, having accomplished forty miles, just at sunset they dropped
their anchor in the still waters which are surrounded by the grand and gloomy cliffs of the Highlands.

The next morning, the river and its shores, were
enveloped in a dense fog, so that one could see but
a few yards before him. Taking advantage of this,
the Indian captives, whom Sir Henry Hudson had

so treacherously ensnared, leaped out of one of the port-holes, and swam ashore.   As soon as they reached the land, they raised loud shouts of hatred and defiance.

The sun soon dispelled the fog, and the voyage was continued, and by night the Half Moon reached a point supposed to be near the present site of Cats-kill Landing.   The natives were numerous, and very friendly.   They came freely on board, apparently unsuspicious of danger.   It was noticeable that there were many very aged men among them.   The river seemed full of fishes, and with their hooks they took large numbers.   The next day the Indians came on board in crowds, bringing pumpkins and tobacco.   The vessel's boats were sent on shore to procure fresh water.

Early the ensuing morning, they pushed up the river five miles, to a point probably near the present city of Hudson.

Sir Henry Hudson does not appear to advantage in the account transmitted to us of this exploration. Mr. Sparks, in his American Biography, gives the following extraordinary account of one of his procedures.

"It is evident that great distrust was entertained by Hudson and his men towards the natives. He now determined to ascertain, by intoxicating

some of the chiefs, and thus throwing them off their
guard, whether they were plotting any treachery.
He accordingly invited several of them into the
cabin, and gave them plenty of brandy to drink.
One of these men had his wife with him, who, the
Journal informs us, ' sate so modestly as any of our
countrywomen would do in a strange place.'   But
the men had less delicacy and were soon quite merry with the brandy.

"One of them, who had been on board from the
first arrival of the ship, was completely intoxicated,
and fell sound asleep, to the great astonishment of
his companions, who probably feared that he had
been poisoned; for they all took to their canoes and
made for the shore, leaving their unlucky comrade
on board. Their anxiety for his welfare soon induced them to return ; and they brought a quantity
of beads, which they gave him, perhaps to enable
him to purchase his freedom from the spell which
had been laid upon him.

"The poor savage slept quietly all night, and
when his friends came to visit him the next morning they found him quite well. This restored their
confidence, so that they came to the ship again in
crowds, in the afternoon, bringing various presents
for Hudson. Their visit which was one of unusual
ceremony is thus described in the Journal :

" ' So at three of the clock in the afternoon, they came aboard and brought tobacco and more beads, and gave them to our master, and made an oration and showed him all the country round about. Then they sent one of their company on land, who presently returned ; and brought a great platter full of venison, dressed by themselves, and they caused him to eat with them. Then they made him reverence and departed, all save the old man that lay aboard.' "

It was now manifest that no northwest passage to the Indies could be found in this direction, and it was not deemed expedient to attempt to ascend the river any farther in the ship. The mate, however, was sent with a boat's crew, to explore the river some distance higher up. It is supposed that the boat ascended several miles above the present site of the city of Albany, Hudson probably going a little beyond where the town of Waterford now is. Upon the return of the boat, the mate having reported that it was useless to attempt any farther ascent of the river with the ship, Sir Henry commenced his return.

Carefully descending the winding channel of the stream, he was so unfortunate as to run the ship on a mud bank, in the middle of the river nearly opposite the present city of Hudson. Without

2

much difficulty the vessel was again floated, having received no injury. But contrary winds detained him upon the spot two days. In the meantime several boat parties visited the banks on both sides of the stream. They were also visited by many of the natives who were unremitting in their kind ness.

A fair wind soon springing up they ran down the river eighteen miles, passing quite a large Indian village where Catskill now stands, and cast anchor in deep water, near Red Hook. Baffled by opposing winds and calms, they slowly worked their way down the stream, the next two days, to near the present point of Castleton. Here a venerable old man, the chief of a small tribe, or rather patriarchal family of forty men and seventeen women, came on board in his birch canoe. He gave Sir Henry a very cordial invitation to visit his little settlement of wigwams, picturesquely nestled upon the banks of the river. Distance lends enchantment to the view. The little hamlet in a sheltered cove where fertile meadows were spread out, was surrounded by fields waving with the harvest. From the deck of the ship the scene presented was one of peace, prosperity and happiness. The smoke ascended gracefully from the wigwam fires, children were sporting upon the beach, and birch canoes, almost as light as bubbles, were being rapidly paddled over the glassy waves.

The good old chief took the English captain ashore and led him into his palace. It was a very humble edifice, constructed of bark so carefully overlapped as effectually to exclude both wind and rain. It was from thirty to forty feet long and eighteen feet wide. There was a door at each end, and ample light was admitted by an opening extending along the whole length, through which the smoke of the fires could escape. The interior was finished with great care, and very smoothly. Under certain states of the atmosphere and of the wind the smoke freely ascended, causing no embarrassment to those within. The ground floor was neatly covered with mats, except in the centre where the fire was built. The whole interior as Sir Hudson entered it, on a serene autumnal day, presented a very cheerful aspect. One might easily be pardoned for imagining, in that hour, that the life of the American savage, free from care, was apparently far more desirable than that of the toil-worn European.

Sir Henry, with the few who accompanied him, was received with great hospitality. Some Indians were immediately sent into the forest for a dinner. They soon returned with some pigeons which they

had shot with their arrows. A nice fat puppy was
also killed, skinned with a clam-shell, and roasted
in the highest style of barbaric culinary art. Thick
mats were provided as seats for the guests at this
royal festival. Hudson was urged to remain all
night. He was evidently a man of very cautious,
if not suspicious temperament. He could not, or
did not conceal, from the Indians his fears that they
were meditating treachery. These artless men, to
convince him that he had nothing to apprehend,
actually broke their bows and arrows, and threw
them into the fire. But nothing could induce Hudson to remain on shore through the night. He describes the land here as very fertile, bearing abun-
dantly, corn, pumpkins, grapes, plums, and various
other kinds of small fruits.

Availing himself of a fair wind, he again spread
his sails, and on the 1st of October, cast anchor at
the mouth of Haverstraw Bay, in the vicinity of
Stony Point. He had scarcely furled his sails, when
a large number of natives came paddling out from
the shore in their little birch canoes. They were
entirely unarmed, bringing apparently in a most
friendly manner, furs, fish and vegetables for sale.
Soon quite a little fleet of these buoyant canoes
were gliding over the water. One Indian, paddling
beneath the cabin windows, and seeing hanging out

certain articles pilfered a pillow and a jacket. As he was making off with his treasures the mate caught sight of him, and seizing his gun mercilessly shot him dead. A severe punishment for so trivial a crime in an untutored savage.

All the Indians on board the Half Moon, as they heard the report of the gun, and saw their unfortunate companion fall dead in his blood, were stricken with terror. Some rushed into their canoes. Others plunged into the river to swim ashore. The vessel's boat immediately put off to pick up the canoe with the stolen goods. As it was returning, a solitary Indian, in the water, probably exhausted and drowning, grasped the gunwale. The cook seized a hatchet and with one blow, deliberately cut off the man's hand at the wrist. The poor creature, uttering a shriek, sank beneath the crimsoned waves and was seen no more.

The next day, the Half Moon descended the river about twenty miles through Tappan Sea, and anchored, it is supposed. near the head of Manhattan island. Sir Henry Hudson was apparently oppressed in some degree with the unjustifiable harshness with which he had treated the simple-hearted, yet friendly natives. He was continually and increasingly apprehensive of treachery. A single canoe containing several men approached the ship.

Hudson's eagle eye perceived that one of these men was one of the captives whom he had seized, but who had escaped from his imprisonment by plunging into the river and swimming ashore. The sight of this man alarmed the captain, and he refused to allow any of them to come on board.

It seems to us rather absurd to suppose that half-a-dozen savages could think of attacking, from a birch canoe, with arrows, a European ship with its well-armed crew. It should be borne in mind that we have the narrative from the white man only. The Indians have had no opportunity to tell their story.

Mr. Brodhead, in his valuable history of New York, gives the following account of the untoward scenes which immediately ensued, compiling from the most ancient records:

"But Hudson, perceiving their intent, would suffer none of them to enter the vessel. Two canoes, full of warriors, then came under the stern, and shot a flight of arrows into the yacht. A few muskets were discharged in retaliation, and two or three of the assailants were killed. Some hundred Indians then assembled at the Point to attack the Half Moon, as she drifted slowly by; but a cannon-shot killed two of them, whereupon the rest fled into the woods. Again the assailants manned another canoe and again the attack was repulsed by a cannon shot which destroyed their frail bark; and so the savages went their way mourning the loss of nine of their warriors. The yacht then got down two leagues beyond that place, and anchored over night on the other side of the river in the bay near Hoboken. Hard by his anchorage and upon that side of the river that is called Mannahatta, Hudson noticed that there was a cliff that looked of the color of white-green. Here he lay wind-bound the next day, and saw no people to trouble him. The following morning, just one month after his arrival at Sandy Hook, Hudson weighed anchor for the last time and coming out of the mouth of the great river, in the which he had run so far, he set all sail and steered off again into the main sea."

It is very evident that Sir Henry Hudson was by no means a good disciplinarian. The authority he exercised over his crew, was very feeble. A mutinous spirit began already to prevail, and we are told that they threatened him savagely. It would appear that Sir Henry and his mate wished to repair to Newfoundland, and after having passed the winter, which was close upon them, there to resume their voyage, in search of a northwest passage, through Davis's Straits. But the turbulent crew would not consent. They compelled the captain to

turn the prow of his ship towards Europe. After
the voyage of a month the Half Moon cast anchor
in the harbor of Dartmouth, England, on the 9th
of November, 1609.

It will be remembered that Sir Henry Hudson
was an Englishman, though he was sailing in the service of the Dutch East India Company.   When the
Dutch Directors heard of his arrival in England, and
of the important discoveries he had made, they sent
orders for him immediately to repair to Amsterdam.
At the same time the Dutch government claimed,
by the right of discovery, all that portion of the
North American continent along whose coasts Hudson had sailed and upon whose shores he had occa-
sionally landed, taking possession of the same in
the name of the Dutch government.

The English government, jealous of the advantage which had thus been gained by the flag of
Holland, peremptorily forbade Hudson to leave his
native country; and for several months the Half
Moon was detained at Dartmouth.

CHAPTER II.

The Progress of Discovery.

Value of the Territory Discovered.—Fate of Hudson.—The Conspiracy.—Aspect of Manhattan Island.—The Trail which has Widened into Broadway.—The Opening Commerce.—The Fur Trade.—Visit of the English Man of War.—Exploring the Sound.—Commercial Enterprise Receives a New Stimulus.—Erection of Forts.—Character of the Fur Trade.

THE Half Moon was detained in England eight months, and did not reach Amsterdam until the summer of 1610. The Dutch Directors, though disappointed in not finding in the region they had explored the much hoped-for Northwest Passage to the Indies, were somewhat elated by the magnificent discoveries which had been made. The territory they claimed, by virtue of these discoveries, extended from the mouth of the Delaware on the South, to Cape Cod on the Northeast. The grand river of Canada, the St. Lawrence, was deemed its northern frontier. Its western boundaries were unexplored and unknown.

This was indeed a princely territory to be owned by any power. The climate was as favorable as any

2*

to be found upon the globe.   The soil was fertile,
the landscape being picturesquely diversified by
mountains and valleys.   Vast forests, of the most
valuable timber, covered immense portions.   Wild
fruits and nuts in great variety were found in profusion.   The territory was watered by several truly
magnificent rivers.   The region was filled with
game ; and furs, of the richest kind and apparently
in exhaustless quantities, could be purchased of the
natives, at an almost nominal price.

It may be worthy of notice, that Sir Henry Hudson never revisited the pleasant region which he
had discovered, and which he had pronounced to
be ' as beautiful a land as the foot of man can tread
upon.'   In the summer of 1610, Hudson entered
the service of a London company and sailed from
the Thames in the " Discovery," in search of either
a Northwest or Northeast passage to the Indies.
Passing Iceland, appropriately so called, he gazed
with astonishment upon Hecla in full eruption,
throwing its fiery flood and molten stones into the
air.   Doubling the Cape of Greenland, he entered
Davis's Straits.   Through these he passed into the
gloomy waters beyond.

' After spending a dismal winter, in the endurance
of great privation, exposed to severe Arctic storms,
his mutinous crew abandoned him, in the midst of

fields of ice, to perish miserably. The following artless account of this tragedy, which is taken from the
lips of one of the mutineers, will be read with interest. The ship was surrounded with ice and the
crew in a starving condition.

"They had been detained at anchor in the ice,"
says Pricket, "about a week, when the first signs of
the mutiny appeared. Green, and Wilson the boat-
swain, came in the night to me, as I was lying in my
berth very lame and told me that they and several of the crew had resolved to seize Hudson and
set him adrift in the boat, with all on board who
were disabled by sickness ; that there were but a
few days' provisions left ; that the master appeared
entirely irresolute, which way to go ; that for themselves they had eaten nothing for three days. Their
only hope therefore was in taking command of the
ship, and escaping from these regions as quickly as
possible.

"I remonstrated with them in the most earnest
manner, entreating them to abandon such a wicked
intention. But all I could say had no effect. It
was decided that the plot should be put into execution at daylight. In the meantime Green went into
Hudson's cabin to keep him company, and to prevent his suspicions from being excited. They had
determined to put the carpenter and John King

into the boat with Hudson and the sick, having some grudge against them for their attachment to the master. King and the carpenter had slept on deck this night, but about daybreak, King was observed to go down into the hold with the cook, who was going for water. Some of the mutineers ran and shut down the hatch over them, while Green and another engaged the attention of the carpenter, so that he did not observe what was going on.

" Hudson now came from the cabin and was immediately seized by Thomas and Bennet, the cook, who had come up from the hold, while Wilson ran behind and bound his arms. He asked them what they meant, and they told him that he would know when he was in the shallop. Hudson called upon the carpenter to help him, telling him that he was bound. But he could render him no assistance being surrounded by mutineers. The boat was now hauled along side, and the sick and lame were called up from their berths. I crawled upon the deck as well as I could and Hudson, seeing me, called to me to come to the hatchway and speak to him.

" I entreated the men, on my knees, for the love of God, to remember their duty. But they only told me to go back to my berth, and would not allow me to have any communication with Hudson. After the captain was put in the boat, the carpenter was set at liberty; but he refused to remain in the ship unless they forced him. So they told him he might go in the boat and allowed him to take his chest with him. Before he got into the boat, he told me that he believed they would soon be taken on board again, as there was no one left who knew enough to bring the ship home. He thought that the boat would be kept in tow. We then took leave of each other, with tears in our eyes, and the carpenter went into the boat, taking a musket and some powder and shot, an iron pot, a small quantity of meal, and other provisions.

" Hudson's son and six of the men were also put into the boat. The sails were then hoisted and they stood eastward, with a fair wind, dragging the shallop from the stern. In a few hours, being clear of the ice, they cut the rope by which the boat was towed, and soon after lost sight of her forever."

The imagination recoils from following the victims thus abandoned, through the long days and nights of lingering death, from hunger and from cold. To God alone has the fearful tragedy been revealed.

The glowing accounts which Sir Henry Hudson had given of the river he had discovered, and particularly of the rich furs there to be obtained, induced the merchants of Amsterdam in the year

1616 to fit out a trading expedition to that region. A
vessel was at once dispatched, freighted with a variety of goods to be exchanged for furs. The enterprise
was eminently successful and gradually more minute information was obtained respecting the territory surrounding the spacious bay into which the
Hudson river empties its flood.

The island of Manhattan, upon which the city
of New York is now built, consisted then of a series
of forest-crowned hills, interspersed with crystal
streamlets and many small but beautiful lakes.
These solitary sheets of water abounded with fish,
and water-fowl of varied plumage. They were fringed with forests, bluffs, and moss-covered rocks. The
upper part of the island was rough, being much broken by storm-washed crags and wild ravines, with
many lovely dells interspersed, fertile in the extreme,
blooming with flowers, and in the season, red with
delicious strawberries. There were also wild grapes
and nuts of various kinds, in great abundance.

The lower part of the island was much more level. There were considerable sections where the
forest had entirely disappeared. The extended
fields, inviting the plough, waved with luxuriant
grass. It was truly a delightful region. The climate was salubrious; the atmosphere in cloudless
transparency rivalled the famed skies of Italy.

Where the gloomy prison of the Tombs now stands, there was a lake of crystal water, overhung by towering trees. Its silence and solitude were disturbed only by the cry of the water-fowl which disported upon its surface, while its depths sparkled with the spotted trout. The lake emptied into the Hudson river by a brook which rippled over its pebbly bed, along the present line of Canal street. This beautiful lake was fed by large springs and was sufficiently deep to float any ship in the navy. Indeed it was some time before its bottom could be reached by any sounding line.

There was a gentle eminence or ridge, forming as it were the backbone of the island, along which there was a narrow trail trodden by the moccasoned feet of the Indian, in single file for countless generations. Here is now found the renowned Broadway, one of the busiest thoroughfares upon the surface of the globe.

On the corner of Grand street and Broadway, there was a well-wooded hill, from whose commanding height one obtained an enchanting view of the whole island with its surrounding waters. Amidst these solitudes there were many valleys in whose peaceful bosoms the weary of other lands seemed to be invited to take refuge.

Indeed it is doubtful whether the whole conti-

nent of North America presented any region more
attractive. The salubrity of its clime, the beauty
of the scenery, the abundance and purity of the waters, the spacious harbor, the luxuriance of the soil
and the unexplored rivers opening communication
with vast and unknown regions of the interior, all
combined in giving to the place charms which could
not be exceeded by any other position on the continent.

The success of the first trading vessel was so
great that, within three years, five other ships were
sent to the " Mauritius river " as the Hudson was
first named. There was thus opened a very brisk
traffic with the Indians which was alike beneficial to
both parties. Soon one or two small forts were
erected and garrisoned on the river for the protection of the traders. Manhattan island, so favorably
situated at the mouth of the river, ere long became
the headquarters of this commerce. Four log
houses were built, it is said, upon the present site
of 39, Broadway.

Here a small company of traders established
themselves in the silence and solitude of the wilderness. Their trading boats ran up the river, and
along the coast, visiting every creek and inlet in the
pursuit of furs. The natives, finding this market
thus suddenly opening before them, and finding that

THE PROGRESS OF DISCOVERY.

their furs, heretofore almost valueless, would purchase for them treasures of civilization of almost
priceless worth, redoubled their zeal in hunting and
trapping.

A small Indian settlement sprang up upon the
spot. Quite large cargoes of furs were collected
during the winter and shipped to Holland in the
spring. The Dutch merchants seem to have been
influenced by a high sentiment of honor. The most
amicable relations existed between them and the
Indians. Henry Christiænsen was the superintendent of this feeble colony. He was a prudent and
just man, and, for some time, the lucrative traffic in
peltry continued without interruption. The Dutch
merchants were exposed to no rivalry, for no European vessels but theirs had, as yet, visited the Mauritius river.

But nothing in this world ever long continues
tranquil. The storm ever succeeds the calm. In
November, of the year 1613, Captain Argal, an Englishman, in a war vessel, looked in upon the little
defenceless trading hamlet, at the mouth of the
Hudson, and claiming the territory as belonging to
England, compelled Christiænsen to avow fealty to
the English crown, and to pay tribute, in token of
his dependence upon that power. Christiænsen
could make no resistance. One broadside from the

British ship would lay his huts in ruins, and expose all the treasures collected there to confiscation. He could only submit to the extortion and send a narrative of the event to the home government.

The merchants in Holland were much alarmed by these proceedings. They presented a petition to the States-General, praying that those who discovered new territory, on the North American continent, or elsewhere, might enjoy the exclusive right of trading with the inhabitants of those regions during six consecutive voyages.

This request was granted, limiting the number of voyages however to four instead of six. In the meantime the Dutch merchants erected and garrisoned two small forts to protect themselves from such piratic excursions as that of captain Argal. In the year 1614 five vessels arrived at Manhattan to transport to Europe the furs which had been purchased. Just as Captain Block was preparing to return, his ship, the Tiger, which was riding at anchor just off the southern point of Manhattan island, took fire, and was burned to the water's edge.

He was a very energetic man, not easily dismayed by misfortune. The island abounded with admirable timber for ship building. He immediately commenced the construction of another vessel. This yacht was forty-four and a half feet long, and eleven and a half feet wide. The natives watched the growth of the stupendous structure with astonishment. In the most friendly manner they rendered efficient aid in drawing the heavy timber from the forest to the shipyard. They also brought in abundant food for the supply of the strangers.

Early in the spring of 1614 the " Restless " was launched. Immediately Captain Block entered upon an exploring tour through what is now called the East River. He gave the whole river the name of the Hellegat, from a branch of the river Scheldt in East Flanders. The unpropitious name still adheres to the tumultuous point of whirling eddies where the waters of the sound unite with those of the river.

Coasting along the narrow portion of the sound, he named the land upon his right, which he did not then know to be an island, Metoac or the Land of Shells. We should rather say he accepted that name from the Indians. On this cruise he discovered the mouths of the Housatonic and of the Connecticut. He ascended this latter stream, which he called Fresh River, several leagues. Indian villages were picturesquely scattered along the shores, and the birch canoes of the Indians were swiftly paddled over the mirrored waters. All else was silence and solitude. The gloom of the forest overshadowed

the banks and the numerous water-fowl were undisturbed upon the stream. The natives were
friendly but timid. They were overawed by the
presence of the gigantic structure which had invaded their solitude.

Continuing his cruise to the eastward he reached
the main ocean, and thus found that the land upon
his left was an island, now known as Long Island.
Still pressing forward he discovered the great Narragansett Bay, which he thoroughly explored, and
then continued his course to Cape Cod, which, it
will be remembered, Sir Henry Hudson had already
discovered, and which he had called New Holland.

Intelligence was promptly transmitted to Holland of these discoveries and the United Company,
under whose auspices the discoveries had been
made, adopted vigorous measures to secure, from
the States-General, the exclusive right to trade with
the natives of those wide realms. A very emphatic
ordinance was passed, granting this request, on the
27th of March, 1614.

This ordinance stimulated to a high degree the
spirit of commercial enterprise. The province was
called New Netherland, and embraced the territory
within the 40th and 45th degrees of north latitude.
All persons, excepting the United " New Netherland
Company," were prohibited from trading within those

limits, under penalty of the confiscation of both vessels and cargoes, and also a fine of fifty thousand Dutch ducats.

The Company immediately erected a trading-house, at the head of navigation of the Hudson river, which as we have mentioned, was then called Prince Maurice's River. This house· was on an island, called Castle Island, a little below the present city of Albany, and was thirty-six feet long and twenty-six feet wide, and was strongly built of logs. As protection from European buccaneers rather than from the friendly Indians, it was surrounded by a strong stockade, fifty feet square. This was encircled by a moat eighteen feet wide. The whole was defended by several cannon and was garrisoned by twelve soldiers.

This port, far away in the loneliness of the wilderness, was called Fort Nassau. Jacob Elkins was placed in command. Now that the majestic Hudson is whitened with the sails of every variety of vessels and barges, while steamers go rushing by, swarming with multitudes, which can scarcely be counted, of the seekers of wealth or pleasures, and railroad trains sweep thundering over the hills and through the valleys, and the landscape is adorned with populous cities and beautiful villas, it is difficult to form a conception of the silence and solitude of those regions but about two hundred and fifty years ago, when the tread of the moccasoned Indian fell noiseless upon the leafy trail, and when the birch canoe alone was silently paddled from cove to cove.

In addition to the fort in the vicinity of Albany, another was erected at the southern extremity of Manhattan Island at the mouth of the Hudson. Here the company established its headquarters and immediately entered into a very honorable and lucrative traffic with the Indians, for their valuable furs. The leaders of the Company were men of integrity, and the Indians were all pleased with the traffic, for they were ever treated with consideration, and received for their furs, which they easily obtained, articles which were of priceless value to them.

The vagabond white men, who were lingering about the frontiers of civilization, inflicting innumerable and nameless outrages upon the natives, were rigorously excluded from these regions. Thus the relations existing between the Indians and their European visitors were friendly in the highest degree. Both parties were alike benefited by this traffic; the Indian certainly not less than the European, for he was receiving into his lowly wigwam the products of the highest civilization.

Indian tribes scattered far and wide through the

primitive and illimitable forest, plied all their energies with new diligence, in taking game. They
climbed the loftiest mountains and penetrated the
most distant streams with their snares. Some came
trudging to the forts on foot, with large packs of
peltries upon their backs. Others came in their
birch canoes, loaded to the gunwales, having set
their traps along leagues of the river's coast and of
distant streams.

Once a year the ships of the company came
laden with the most useful articles for traffic with
the Indians, and, in return, transported back to
Europe the furs which had been collected. Such
were the blessings which peace and friendship conferred upon all. There seemed to be no temptation
to outrage. The intelligent Hollanders were well
aware that it was for their interest to secure the
confidence of the Indian by treating him justly.
And the Indian was not at all disposed to incur the
resentment of strangers from whom he was receiving
such great benefits.

The little yacht "Restless," of which we have
spoken, on one of her exploring tours, visited Delaware Bay, and ascended that beautiful sheet of
water as far as the Schuylkill River. Runners were
also sent back from the forts, to follow the narrow
trails far into the woods, to open communication

with new tribes, to examine the country, and to
obtain a more intimate acquaintance with the manners and customs of the Indians.

In the spring of 1617 a very high freshet, accompanied by the breaking up of the ice, so injured
Fort Nassau that the traders were compelled to
abandon it. A new and very advantageous situation
was selected, at the mouth of the Tawasentha
Creek, subsequently called Norman's Kill. This
name is said to have been derived from a native of
Denmark, called the Norman, who settled there in
1630.

In this vicinity there was a very celebrated confederation of Indian tribes called the Five Nations.
These tribes were the Mohawks, Oneidas, Onon-
dagas, Cayugas and Senecas. They were frequently
known by the generic name of the Iroquois. When
the Dutch arrived, the Iroquois were at war with
the Canadian Indians, who, though composed of
different tribes, were known by the general name of
the Algonquins. The Iroquois had been worsted in
several conflicts. This led them eagerly to seek
alliance with the white men, who, with their wonderful instruments of war, seemed to wield the energies of thunder and lightning.

The Algonquins had, some years before, formed
an alliance with the French in Canada. The Iro-

quois now entered into an alliance with the Dutch.
It was a very important movement, and the treaty
took place, with many surroundings of barbaric
pomp, on the banks of the Norman's Kill.

Ambassadors from each of the five tribes graced
the occasion. Leading chiefs of several other tribes
were also invited to be present, to witness the imposing ceremony. The garrison furnished for the
pageant the waving of silken banners and the exhil-
arating music of its band. The Indian chiefs attended with their decorated weapons, and they were
arrayed in the richest costume of war paint, fringed
garments, and nodding plumes.

The assembly was large. The belt of peace,
gorgeously embroidered with many-colored beads, on
softly-tanned deer skin, was held at one end by the
Iroquois chieftains, and at the other by the prominent men of the Dutch Company, in their most
showy attire. The pipe of peace was smoked with
solemn gravity. The tomahawk was buried, and
each party pledged itself to eternal friendship.

The united nation of the Iroquois, in numbers
and valor, had become quite supreme throughout
all this region. All the adjacent tribes bowed
before their supremacy. In Mr. Street's metrical
romance, entitled " Frontenac," he speaks, in pleas-

ing verse, of the prowess and achievements of these
formidable warriors.

> " The fierce Adirondacs had fled from their wrath,
> The Hurons been swept from their merciless path,
> Around, the Ottawas, like leaves, had been strown,
> And the lake of the Eries struck silent and lone.
> The Lenape, lords once of valley and hill,
> Made women, bent low at their conquerors' will.
> By the far Mississippi the Illini shrank
> When the trail of the Tortoise was seen on the bank.
> On the hills of New England the Pequod turned pale
> When the howl of the Wolf swelled at night on the gale,
> And the Cherokee shook, in his green smiling bowers,
> When the foot of the Bear stamped his carpet of flowers."

Thus far the Iroquois possessed only bows and
arrows. They were faithful to their promises, and
implicit confidence could be reposed in their pledge.
The Dutch traders, without any fear, penetrated the
wilderness in all directions, and were invariably hospitably received in the wigwams of the Indians.

In their traffic the Dutch at first exchanged for
furs only articles of ornament or of domestic value.
But the bullet was a far more potent weapon in the
chase and in the hunting-field than the arrow. The
Indians very soon perceived the vast advantage they
would derive in their pursuit of game, from the
musket, as well as the superiority it would give
them over all their foes. They consequently became very eager to obtain muskets, powder and
ball. They were warm friends of the Europeans.

There seemed to be no probability of their becoming enemies. Muskets and steel traps enabled them to obtain many more furs. Thus the Indians were soon furnished with an abundant supply of fire-arms, and became unerring marksmen.

Year after year the returns from the trading-posts became more valuable; and the explorations were pushed farther and farther into the interior. The canoes of the traders penetrated the wide realms watered by the upper channels of the Delaware. A trading-house was also erected in the vast forest, upon the Jersey shore of the Hudson River, where the thronged streets of Jersey City at the present hour cover the soil.

We have now reached the year 1618, two years before the arrival of the Pilgrims at Plymouth. Though the energetic Dutch merchants were thus perseveringly and humanely pushing their commerce, and extending their trading posts, no attempt had yet been made for any systematic agricultural colonization.

The Dutch alone had then any accurate knowledge of the Hudson River, or of the coasts of Connecticut, Rhode Island, and Long Island. In 1618 the special charter of the Company, conferring upon them the monopoly of exclusive trade with the Indians, expired. Though the trade was thus thrown open to any adventurous Dutch merchant, still the members of the Company enjoyed an immense advantage in having all the channels perfectly understood by them, and in being in possession of such important posts.

English fishing vessels visited the coast of Maine, and an unsuccessful attempt had been made to establish a colony at the mouth of the Kennebec River. Sir Walter Raleigh had also made a very vigorous but unavailing effort to establish a colony in Virginia. Before the year 1600, every vestige of his attempt had disappeared. Mr. John Romeyn Brodhead, in his valuable history of the State of New York, speaking of this illustrious man, says:

"The colonists, whom Raleigh sent to the island of Roanoke in 1585, under Grenville and Lane, returned the next year dispirited to England. A second expedition, dispatched in 1587, under John White, to found the borough of Raleigh, in Virginia, stopped short of the unexplored Chesapeake, whither it was bound, and once more occupied Roanoke. In 1590 the unfortunate emigrants had wholly disappeared; and with their extinction all immediate attempts to establish an English colony in Virginia were abandoned. Its name alone survived.

"After impoverishing himself in unsuccessful

efforts to add an effective American plantation to his native kingdom, Raleigh, the magnanimous patriot, was consigned, under an unjust judgment, to lingering imprisonment in the Tower of London, to be followed, after the lapse of fifteen years, by a still more iniquitous execution. Yet returning justice has fully vindicated Raleigh's fame. And nearly two centuries after his death the State of North Carolina gratefully named its capital after that extraordinary man, who united in himself as many kinds of glory as were ever combined in any individual."

CHAPTER III.

The Commencement of Colonization.

The Puritans.—Memorial to the States-General.—Disagreement of
the English and the Dutch.—Colony on the Delaware.—Purchase
of Manhattan.—The First Settlement.—An Indian Robbed and
Murdered.— Description of the Island.— Diplomatic Intercourse.—Testimony of De Rassieres.—The Patroons.—The Disaster at Swaanendael.

IN the year 1620 the Puritans founded their
world-renowned colony at Plymouth, as we have
minutely described in the History of Miles Standish.
It will be remembered that the original company of
Puritans were of English birth. Dissatisfied with
the ritual and ceremonies which the Church of
England had endeavored to impose upon them, they
had emigrated to Holland, where they had formed a
church upon their own model. Rev. John Robinson,
a man of fervent piety and of enlightened views
above his times, was their pastor.

After residing in Holland for several years, this
little band of Englishmen, not pleased with that
country as their permanent abode, decided to seek a
new home upon the continent of North America.

They first directed their attention towards Virginia, but various obstacles were thrown in their way by the British Government, and at length Mr. Robinson addressed a letter to the Dutch Company, intimating the disposition felt by certain members of his flock, to take up their residence at New Netherland.

The proposition was very cordially received. The intelligent gentlemen of that Company at once saw that there was thus presented to them an opportunity to establish a colony, at their trading post, which it would be wise to embrace.   They therefore addressed a memorial upon the subject to the States-General, and to the Prince of Orange, in which they urged the importance of accepting the proposition which they had received from Mr. Robinson, and of thus commencing an agricultural colony upon the island of Manhattan.   In this memorial they write under date of February, 1620:

" It now happens that there resides at Leyden an English clergyman, well versed in the Dutch language, who is favorably inclined to go and dwell there.   Your petitioners are assured that he knows more than four hundred families, who, provided they were defended and secured there by your Royal Highness, and that of the High and Mighty Lords States-General, from all violence on the part of other potentates, would depart thither, with him, from this country and from England, to plant, forthwith, everywhere the true and pure christian religion; to instruct the Indians of those countries in the true doctrine; to bring them to the christian belief; and likewise, through the grace of the Lord, and for the greater honor of the rulers of this land to people all that region under a new dispensation; all under the order and command of your princely Highness and of the High and Mighty Lords States-General.

"Your petitioners have also learned that His Britannic Majesty is inclined to people the aforesaid lands with Englishmen; to destroy your petitioners' possessions and discoveries, and also to deprive this State of its right to these lands, while the ships belonging to this country, which are there during the whole of the present year, will apparently and probably be surprised by the English."

The petitioners therefore prayed that the request of Mr. Robinson might be favorably regarded; that the contemplated colony should be taken under the protection of the Dutch government, and that two ships of war should be sent out for the defence of the infant settlements.

The Dutch government was then upon the eve of a war with Spain, and all its energies were demanded in preparation for the conflict. They therefore quite peremptorily refused to entertain the petition of the New Netherland Company. Thus the destination of the Puritans was changed. Though they were not encouraged to commence their colonial life at New Netherland, still it was their intention when they sailed from England, to find a home somewhere in that vicinity, as England, as well as Holland, claimed the whole coast. A note, in the History of New Netherland, by E. B. O'Callaghan, contains the following interesting statement upon this subject :

"Some historians represent that the Pilgrims were taken against their will to New Plymouth, by the treachery of the captain of the Mayflower, who, they assert, was bribed by the Dutch to land them at a distance from the Hudson river. This has been shown, over and over again, to have been a calumny; and, if any farther evidence were requisite, it is now furnished, of a most conclusive nature, by the petition in behalf of the Rev. Mr. Robinson's congregation, of Feb. 1620, and the rejection of its prayer by their High Mightinesses.

" That the Dutch were anxious to secure the settlement of the Pilgrims under them, is freely admitted by the latter. Governor Bradford, in his History of the Plymouth Colony, acknowledges it, and adds that the Dutch for that end made them large offers.

3*

"Winslow corroborates this in his 'Brief Narrative,' and adds that the Dutch would have freely transported us to the Hudson river, and furnished every family with cattle. The whole of this evidence satisfactorily establishes the good will of the Dutch people towards the English; while the determination of the States-General proves that there was no encouragement held out by the Dutch government to induce them to settle in their American possessions. On the contrary, having formally rejected their petition, they thereby secured themselves against all suspicion of dealing unfairly by those who afterwards landed at Cape Cod. It is to be hoped, therefore, that even for the credit of the Pilgrims, the idle tale will not be repeated."

There were many indications that a conflict would ere long arise between the Dutch and the English. The English repudiated entirely the Dutch claim to any right of possession on the Atlantic coast. They maintained their right to the whole American coast, from the Spanish possessions in Florida, to the French posts in Canada. The English government founded its claim upon the ground of first discovery, occupation and possession. Various companies, in England, had, by charters and letters patent from their sovereigns, been entrusted with these vast territories. It was quite evident that these conflicting claims between England and Holland must eventually lead to collision.

The Dutch merchants continued to push their commercial enterprises in New Netherland with great energy. They were preparing to send quite a large fleet of merchant vessels to the extensive line of coast which they claimed, when the British merchants composing what was called the Plymouth Company, took the alarm, and presented a petition to James I., remonstrating against such proceedings. The British government promptly sent an ambassador to Holland to urge the States-General to prohibit the departure of the fleet, and to forbid the establishment of a Dutch colony in those regions. The diplomacy which ensued led to no decisive results.

In the year 1623, the Dutch sent a ship, under captain May, and established a small colony upon the eastern banks of the Delaware, about fifty miles from its mouth. The settlement, which consisted of about thirty families, was in the vicinity of the present town of Gloucester. A fortress was erected, called Fort Nassau. This was the first European settlement upon the Delaware, which stream was then called Prince Hendrick's, or South River. Another fortified post, called Fort Orange, was established upon the western banks of the Hudson

River about thirty-six miles from the island of Manhattan.

Very slowly the tide of emigration began to flow towards the Hudson. A few families settled on Staten Island. Not pleased with their isolated location, they soon removed to the northern shore of Long Island, and reared their log cabins upon the banks of a beautiful bay, which they called Wahle-Bocht, or " the Bay of the Foreigners." The name has since been corrupted into Wallabout. The western extremity of Long Island was then called Breukelen, which has since been Anglicised into Brooklyn.

The government of these feeble communities was committed to a Governor, called Director, and a Council of five men. One of the first Governors was Peter Minuit, who was appointed in the year 1624. The English still claimed the territory which the Dutch were so quietly and efficiently settling. In the year 1626, the Dutch decided to make a permanent settlement upon Manhattan island, which was then estimated to contain about twenty-two thousand acres of land. The island was purchased of the natives for twenty-four dollars. It was all that, at that time, the savage wilderness was worth. In that year the export of furs amounted to nineteen thousand dollars.

The colony soon numbered about two hundred persons. The village consisted of thirty log houses, extending along the banks of the East River. These cabins were one story high, with thatched roof, wooden chimneys, and two rooms on the floor. Barrels, placed on an end, furnished the tables. The chairs were logs of wood. Undoubtedly in many of these humble homes more true happiness was found than is now experienced in some of the palatial mansions which grace the gorgeous avenues of the city. About this time three ships arrived, containing a large number of families with farming implements, and over a hundred head of cattle. To prevent the cattle from being lost in the woods, they were pastured on Governor's, then called Nutten's Island.

And now the tide of emigration began pretty rapidly to increase. The Dutch transported emigrants for twelve and a half cents a day, during the voyage, for both passage and food. They also gave them, upon reaching the colony, as much land as they were able to cultivate. With a wise toleration, which greatly honored them, the fullest religious freedom of speech and worship was allowed.

A strong block-house, surrounded with palisades of red cedar, was thrown up on the south point of Manhattan Island, and was called Fort Amsterdam. This became the headquarters of the government and the capital of the extended, though not very clearly defined, realm of New Netherland.

An unfortunate occurrence now took place which eventually involved the colony in serious trouble. An Indian, from the vicinity of Westchester, came with his nephew, a small boy, bringing some beaver skins to barter with the Dutch at the fort. The narrow trail through the forest, led in a southeast direction, along the shore of the East River, till it reached what was called Kip's Bay. Then, diverging to the west, it passed near the pond of fresh water, which was about half way between what are now Broadway and Chatham streets. This pond, for a century or more, was known as the Kolck or the Collect.

When the Indians reached this point, they were waylaid by three white men, robbed of their furs, and the elder one was murdered. The boy made his escape and returned to his wilderness home, vowing to revenge the murder of his uncle. It does not appear that the Dutch authorities were informed of this murder. They certainly did not punish the murderers, nor make any attempt to expiate the crime, by presents to the Indians.

"The island of Manhattan," wrote De Rassieres at this time, "is full of trees and in the middle rocky. On the north side there is good land in two places, where two farmers, each with four horses, would have enough to do without much grubbing or clearing at first. The grass is good in the forests and valleys; but when made into hay, it is not so nutritious for the cattle as the hay in Holland, in consequence of its wild state, yet it annually improves by culture.

"On the east side there rises a large level field, of about one hundred and sixty acres, through which runs a very fine fresh stream; so that land can be ploughed without much clearing. It appears to be good. The six farms, four of which lie along the river Hell-gate, stretching to the south side of the island, have at least one hundred and twenty acres to be sown with winter seed, which, at the most, may have been ploughed eight times."

There were eighteen families at Fort Orange, which was situated on Tawalsoutha creek, on the west side of the Hudson river, about thirty-six Dutch miles above the island of Manhattan. These colonists built themselves huts of bark, and lived on terms of cordial friendship with the Indians. Wassenaar writes, "The Indians were as quiet as lambs, and came and traded with all the freedom imaginable."

The Puritans had now been five years at Plymouth. So little were they acquainted with the

geography of the country that they supposed New
England to be an island.* Floating rumors had
reached them of the Dutch colony at the mouth of
the Hudson. Governor Bradford commissioned Mr.
Winslow to visit the Dutch, who had sent a ship
to Narragansett bay to trade, that he might dissuade them from encroaching in their trade upon territory which the Puritans considered as exclusively
belonging to them. Mr. Winslow failed to meet the
Dutch before their vessel had sailed on its return to
Manhattan.

Soon after this the Dutch Governor, Peter
Minuit, sent secretary De Rässieres to Governor
Bradford, with a very friendly letter, congratulating
the Plymouth colony upon its prosperity, inviting to
commercial relations, and offering to supply their
English neighbors with any commodities which they
might want.

Governor Bradford, in his reply, very cordially
reciprocated these friendly greetings. Gracefully he
alluded to the hospitality with which the exiled Pilgrims had been received in Holland. "Many of
us," he wrote, "are tied by the good and courteous
entreaty which we have found in your country,
having lived there many years with freedom and
good content, as many of our friends do this day;

* Winslow in Young (p. 371).

for which we are bound to be thankful, and our children after us, and shall never forget the same."

At the same time he claimed that the territory, north of forty degrees of latitude, which included a large part of New Netherland, and all their Hudson river possessions, belonged to the English. Still he promised that, for the sake of good neighborhood, the English would not molest the Dutch at the mouth of the Hudson, if they would " forbear to trade with the natives in this bay and river of Narragansett and Sowames, which is, as it were, at our doors."

The authorities at Fort Amsterdam could not, for a moment, admit this claim of English supremacy over New Netherland. Director Minuit returned an answer, remarkable for its courteous tone, but in which he firmly maintained the right of the Dutch to trade with the Narragansetts as they had done for years, adding "As the English claim authority under the king of England, so we derive ours from the States of Holland, and we shall defend it."

Governor Bradford sent this correspondence to England. In an accompanying document he said, "the Dutch, for strength of men and fortification, far exceed us in all this land. They have used trading here for six or seven and twenty years ; but have begun to plant of later time ; and now have re-

duced their trade to some order, and confined it
only to their company, which, heretofore, was spoil-
ed by their seamen and interlopers, as ours is, this
year most notoriously. Besides spoiling our trade,
the Dutch continue to sell muskets, powder and shot
to the Indians, which will be the overthrow of all, if
it be not looked into."

Director Minuit must have possessed some very
noble traits of character. After waiting three
months to receive a reply to his last communication,
he sent another letter, reiterating the most friendly
sentiments, and urging that an authorized agent
should be sent from Plymouth to New Amsterdam,
to confer "by word of mouth, touching our mutual
commerce and trading." He stated, moreover, that
if it were inconvenient for Governor Bradford to
send such an agent, they would depute one to Plymouth themselves. In further token of kindness, he
sent to the Plymouth Governor, "a rundlet of sugar
and two Holland cheeses."

It is truly refreshing to witness the fraternal
spirit manifested on this occasion. How many of
the woes of this world might have been averted
had the brotherhood of man been thus recognized
by the leaders of the nations!

A messenger was sent to Plymouth. He was
hospitably entertained, and returned to Fort Am-

sterdam with such testimonials of his reception as induced Director Minuit to send a formal ambassador to Plymouth, entrusted with plenipotentiary powers. Governor Bradford apologized for not sending an ambassador to Fort Amsterdam, stating, "one of our boats is abroad, and we have much business at home." Director Minuit selected Isaac De Rassieres, secretary of the province, "a man of fair and genteel behavior," as his ambassador. This movement was, to those infant colonies, an event of as much importance as any of the more stately embassies which have been interchanged between European courts.

The barque Nassau was fitted out, and manned with a small band of soldiers, and some trumpeters. It was the last of September, 1629, when earth and sky were bathed in all the glories of New England autumnal days. In De Rassieres' account of the excursion, he writes:

"Sailing through Hell-gate, and along the shores of Connecticut and Rhode Island, we arrived, early the next month, off Frenchman's Point, at a small river where those of New Plymouth have a house, made of hewn oak planks, called Aptuxet; where they keep two men, winter and summer, in order to maintain the trade and possession."

This Aptuxet was at the head of Buzzard's Bay,

upon the site of the present village of Monumet, in
the town of Sandwich.   Near by there was a creek,
penetrating the neck of Cape Cod, which approached another creek on the other side so near that, by
a portage of but about five miles, goods could be
transported across.

As the Nassau came in sight of this lonely trading port suddenly the peals of the Dutch trumpets
awoke the echoes of the forest.   It was the 4th of
October.   A letter was immediately dispatched by
a fleet-footed Indian runner to Plymouth.   A boat
was promptly sent to the head of the creek, called
Manoucusett, on the north side of the cape, and De
Rassieres, with his companions, having threaded the
Indian trail through the wilderness for five miles,
was received on board the Pilgrims' boat and conveyed to Plymouth, " honorably attended with the
noise of trumpeters." *

This meeting was a source of enjoyment to both
parties.   The two nations of England and Holland
were in friendly alliance, and consequently this
interview, in the solitudes of the New World, of the
representatives of the two colonies, was mutually
agreeable.   The Pilgrims, having many of them
for a long time resided in Holland, cherished memories of that country with feelings of strong affection,

* Bradford in Prince, 248.

and regarded the Hollanders almost as fellow-coun-trymen.

But again Governor Bradford asserted the right of the English to the country claimed by the Dutch, and even intimated that force might soon be employed to vindicate the British pretentions. We must admire the conduct of both parties in this emergency. The Dutch, instead of retaliating with threats and violence, sent a conciliatory memorial to Charles I., then King of England. And Charles, much to his credit, issued an order that all the English ports, whether in the kingdom or in the terri-tories of the British king, should be thrown open to the Dutch vessels, trading to or from New Nether-land.

The management of the affairs of the Dutch Colony was entrusted to a body of merchants called the West India Company. In the year 1629, this energetic company purchased of the Indians the exclusive title to a vast territory, extending north from Cape Henlopen, on the south side of Delaware Bay, two miles in breadth and running thirty-two miles inland.

The reader of the record of these days, often meets with the word *Patroon*, without perhaps having any very distinct idea of its significance. In order to encourage emigration and the establishment of colonies, the authorities in Holland issued a charter, conferring large extents of land and exclusive privileges, upon such members of the West India Company as might undertake to settle any colony in New Netherland.

"All such," it was proclaimed in this charter, "shall be acknowledged *Patroons* of New Netherland, who shall, within the space of four years, undertake to plant a colony there of fifty souls upwards of fifteen years of age. The Patroons, by virtue of their power, shall be permitted, at such places as they shall settle their colonies, to extend their limits four miles* along the shore, and so far into the country as the situation of the occupiers will admit." The patroons, thus in possession of territory equal to many of the dukedoms and principalities of Europe, were invested with the authority which had been exercised in Europe by the old feudal lords. They could settle all disputes, in civil cases, between man and man. They could appoint local officers and magistrates, erect courts, and punish all crimes committed within their limits, being ever authorized to inflict death upon the gallows. They could purchase any amount of unappropriated lands from the Indians.

One of these patroons, Kiliaen Van Rensselaer

* Dutch miles, equal to sixteen English miles.

a wealthy merchant in Holland, who had been accustomed to polish pearls and diamonds, became, as patroon, possessed of nearly the whole of the present counties of Albany and Rensselaer, in the State of New York, embracing the vast area of one thousand one hundred and forty-one square miles. Soon all the important points on the Hudson River and the Delaware were thus caught up by these patroons, wealthy merchants of the West India Company.

When the news of these transactions reached Holland, great dissatisfaction was felt by the less fortunate shareholders, that individuals had grasped such a vast extent of territory. It was supposed that Director Minuit was too much in sympathy with the patroons, who were becoming very powerful, and he was recalled. All were compelled to admit that during his administration the condition of the colony had been prosperous. The whole of Manhattan Island had been honestly purchased of the Indians. Industry had flourished. Friendly relations were everywhere maintained with the natives. The northwestern shores of Long Island were studded with the log cottages of the settlers. During his directorship the exports of the colony had trebled, amounting, in the year 1632, to nearly fifty thousand dollars.

We come now to a scene of war, blood and woe,

for which the Dutch were not at all accountable. It will be remembered that a colony had been established near the mouth of Delaware Bay. Two vessels were dispatched from Holland for this point containing a number of emigrants, a large stock of cattle, and whaling equipments, as whales abounded in the bay. The ship, called the Walvis, arrived upon the coast in April, 1631. Running along the western shore of this beautiful sheet of water, they came to a fine navigable stream, which was called Horekill, abounding with picturesque islands, with a soil of exuberant fertility, and where the waters were filled with fishes and very fine oysters. There was here also a roadstead unequalled in the whole bay for convenience and safety.

Here the emigrants built a fort and surrounded it with palisades, and a thriving Dutch colony of about thirty souls was planted. They formally named the place, which was near the present town of Lewiston, Swaanendael. A pillar was raised, surmounted by a plate of glittering tin, upon which was emblazoned the arms of Holland; and which also announced that the Dutch claimed the territory by the title of discovery, purchase and occupation.

For a while the affairs of this colony went on very prosperously. But in May, 1632, an expedition, consisting of two ships, was fitted out from Holland, with additional emigrants and supplies. Just before the vessels left the Texel, a ship from Manhattan brought the melancholy intelligence to Amsterdam that the colony at Swaanendael had been destroyed by the savages, thirty-two men having been killed outside of the fort working in the fields. Still DeVrees, who commanded the expedition, hoping that the report was exaggerated, and that the colony might still live, in sadness and disappointment proceeded on his way. One of his vessels ran upon the sands off Dunkirk, causing a delay of two months. It was not until the end of December that the vessels cast anchor off Swaanendael. No boat from the shore approached; no signs of life met the eye. The next morning a boat, thoroughly armed, was sent into the creek on an exploring tour.

Upon reaching the spot where the fort had been erected they found the building and palisades burned, and the ground strewn with the bones of their murdered countrymen, intermingled with the remains of cattle. The silence and solitude of the tombs brooded over the devastated region. Not even a savage was to be seen. As the boat returned with these melancholy tidings, DeVrees caused a heavy cannon to be fired, hoping that its thunders, reverberating over the bay, and echoing through the trails of the wilderness, might reach the ear of some friendly Indian, from whom he could learn the details of the disaster.

The next morning a smoke was seen curling up from the forest near the ruins. The boat was again sent into the creek, and two or three Indians were seen cautiously prowling about. But mutual distrust stood in the way of any intercourse. The Dutch were as apprehensive of ambuscades and the arrows of the Indians, as were the savages of the bullets of the formidable strangers.

Some of the savages at length ventured to come down to the shore, off which the open boat floated, beyond the reach of arrows. Lured by friendly signs, one of the Indians soon became emboldened to venture on board. He was treated with great kindness, and succeeded in communicating the following, undoubtedly true, account of the destruction of the colony:

One of the chiefs, seeing the glittering tin plate, emblazoned with the arms of Holland, so conspicuously exposed upon the column, apparently without any consciousness that he was doing anything wrong, openly, without any attempt at secrecy, took it down and quite skilfully manufactured it into tobacco pipes. The commander of the fort, a man by the name of Hossett, complained so bitterly of this, as an outrage that must not pass unavenged, that some of the friendly Indians, to win his favor, killed the chief, and brought to Hossett his head, or some other decisive evidence that the deed was done.

The commandant was shocked at this severity of retribution, so far exceeding anything which he had desired, and told the savages that they had done very wrong; that they should only have arrested the chief and brought him to the fort. The commandant would simply have reprimanded him and forbidden him to repeat the offence.

The ignorant Indians of the tribe, whose chief had thus summarily, and, as they felt, unjustly been put to death, had all their savage instincts roused to intensity. They regarded the strangers at the fort as instigating the deed and responsible for it. They resolved upon bloody vengeance.

A party of warriors, thoroughly armed, came stealing through the glades of the forest and approached the unsuspecting fort. All the men were at work in the fields excepting one, who was left sick at home. There was also chained up in the fort, a powerful and faithful mastiff, of whom the Indians stood in great dread. Three of the savages, concealing, as far as they could, their weapons, approached the fort, under the pretence of bartering some beaver skins. They met Hossett, the commander, not far from the door. He entered the house with them, not having the slightest suspicion of their hostile intent. He ascended some steep stairs into the attic, where the stores for trade were deposited, and as he was coming down, one of the Indians, watching his opportunity, struck him dead with an axe. They then killed the sick man. Standing at a cautious distance, they shot twenty-five arrows into the chained mastiff till he sank motionless in death.

The colonists in the field, in the meantime, were entirely unaware of the awful scenes which were transpiring, and of their own impending peril. The wily Indians approached them, under the guise of friendship. Each party had its marked man. At a given signal, with the utmost ferocity they fell upon their victims. With arrows, tomahawks and war-clubs, the work was soon completed. Not a man escaped.

CHAPTER IV.

The Administration of Van Twiller.

DE VREES very wisely decided that it would be
but a barren vengeance to endeavor to retaliate
upon the roaming savages, when probably more suffering would be inflicted upon the innocent than
upon the guilty. He therefore, to their astonishment and great joy, entered into a formal treaty of
peace and alliance with them. Any attempt to bring
the offenders to justice would of course have been
unavailing, as they could easily scatter, far and wide,
through the trackless wilderness. Arrangements
were made for re-opening trade, and the Indians
with alacrity departed to hunt beaver.

A new Director was appointed at Manhattan,
Wouter Van Twiller. He was an inexperienced young

man, and owed his appointment to the powerful pa-
tronage he enjoyed from having married the niece
of the patroon Van Rensselaer. Thus a "raw Amsterdam clerk," embarked in a ship of twenty guns,
with a military force of one hundred and four soldiers, to assume the government of New Netherland. The main object of this mercantile governor
seemed to be to secure trade with the natives and
to send home furs.

De Vrees, having concluded his peace with the Indians, sailed up the South river, as they then called
the Delaware, through the floating ice, to a trading
post, which had been established some time before
at a point about four miles below the present site
of Philadelphia. He thought he saw indications of
treachery, and was constantly on his guard. He
found the post, which was called Fort Nassau, like
a similar post on the Hudson, deserted. The chiefs,
however, of nine different tribes, came on board,
bringing presents of beaver skins, avowing the most
friendly feelings, and they entered into a formal
treaty with the Dutch. There did not, however,
seem to be any encouragement again to attempt the
establishment of a colony, or of any trading posts
in that region. He therefore abandoned the Delaware river, and for some time no further attempts
were made to colonize its coasts.

In April, 1633, an English ship arrived at Manhattan. The bluff captain, Jacob Elkins, who had formerly been in the Dutch employ, but had been dismissed from their service, refused to recognize the Dutch authorities, declaring that New Netherland was English territory, discovered by Hudson, an Englishman. It was replied that though Hudson was an Englishman, he was in the service of the East India Company at Amsterdam; that no English colonists had ever settled in the region, and that the river itself was named Mauritius river, after the Prince of Orange.

Elkins was not to be thus dissuaded. He had formerly spent four years at this post, and was thoroughly acquainted with the habits and language of the Indians. His spirit was roused. He declared that he would sail up the river if it cost him his life. Van Twiller was equally firm in his refusal. He ordered the Dutch flag to be run up at fort Amsterdam, and a salute to be fired in honor of the Prince of Orange. Elkins, in retaliation, unfurled the English flag at his mast-head, and fired a salute in honor of King Charles. After remaining a week at fort Amsterdam, and being refused a license to ascend the river, he defiantly spread his colors to the breeze, weighed anchor, and boldly sailed up the stream to fort Orange. This was the first British vessel which ascended the North river.

The pusillanimous Van Twiller was in a great rage, but had no decision of character to guide him in such an emergency. The merchant clerk, invested with gubernatorial powers, found himself in waters quite beyond his depth. He collected all the people of the fort, broached a cask of wine, and railed valiantly at the intrepid Englishman, whose ship was fast disappearing beyond the palisades. His conduct excited only the contempt and derision of those around.

DeVrees was a man of very different fibre. He had, but a few days before, entered the port from Swaanendael. He dined with the Governor that day, and said to him in very intelligible Dutch :

" You have committed a great folly. Had it been my case, I would have helped the Englishman to some eight pound iron beans, and have prevented him from going up the river. The English are of so haughty a nature that they think that everything belongs to them. I would immediately send a frigate after him, and drive him out of the river."

Stimulated by this advice, Van Twiller prepared, as speedily as possible, three well armed vessels, strongly manned with soldiers, and sent them, under

an intrepid captain, in pursuit of the intruders.
They found the English ship, the William, about a
mile below fort Orange.   A tent was pitched upon
the shore, where, for a fortnight, the English had
been pursuing a very lucrative traffic for furs.   The
Dutch soldiers were in strength which Elkins could
not resist.

They ordered him to strike his tent.   He refused.
They did it for him; reshipped all his goods which
he had transferred to the shore, to trade. with the
Indians, and also the furs which he had purchased.
They then weighed the anchors of the William, unfurled her sails, and, with trumpet blasts of victory,
brought the ship, captain and crew down to fort
Amsterdam.   The ship was then convoyed to sea,
and the discomfited Elkins returned to London.
Thus terminated, in utter failure, the first attempt
of the English to enter into trade with the Indians
of New Netherland.

The Dutch were now the only Europeans who
had occupied any part of the present territory of
New York, New Jersey, Pennsylvania and Delaware.
They were also carrying on a very flourishing trade
with the Indians on the Connecticut river, which
was then called Fresh river, and this " long before
any English had dreamed of going there."   The
value of this traffic may be inferred from the fact

4*

that, in the year 1633, sixteen thousand beaver skins were sent to Holland from the North river alone.

To strengthen their title, thus far founded on discovery and exclusive visitation, the Dutch, in 1632, purchased of the Indians nearly all of the lands on both sides of the Connecticut river, including Saybrook Point, at the mouth, where the arms of the States-General were affixed to a tree in token of possession. A fort was also commenced, near the mouth of the river, and a trading post established some miles up the stream, at the point now occupied by the city of Hartford.

About the same time, Lord Warwick, assuming that a legitimate grant of the region had been made to him by the king of England, conveyed to Lords Say, Brook and others, all the territory running southwest from Narragansett river, to the distance of one hundred and twenty miles along the coast, and reaching back, through the whole breadth of the country, from the Western Ocean to the South Sea. The geography of these regions was then very imperfectly known. No one had any conception of the vast distance between the Atlantic Ocean and the shores of the Pacific. The trading post, which the Dutch had established on the Connecticut, was called Fort Hope.

As soon as it was known, at Plymouth and Boston, that the Dutch had taken formal possession of the valley of the Connecticut, Governor Winslow hastened to confer with the Massachusetts Governor respecting their duties. As it was doubtful whether the region of the Connecticut was embraced within either of their patents, they decided not to interfere. But through diplomatic policy they assigned a different reason for their refusal.

"In regard," said Governor Winthrop, "that the place was not fit for plantation, there being three or four thousand warlike Indians, and the river not to be gone into but by small pinnaces, having a bar affording but six feet at high water, and for that no vessel can get in for seven months in the year, partly by reason of the ice, and then the violent stream, we thought not fit to meddle with it."*

Still Governor Winthrop looked wistfully towards the Connecticut. Though he admitted that the lower part of the valley was "out of the claim of the Massachusetts patent," it could not be denied that the upper part of the valley was included in their grant. In the summer of 1633, John Oldham, with three companions, penetrated the wilderness, through the Indian trails, one hundred and sixty miles to the Connecticut river. They were hospita-

* Morton's memorial, page 176.

bly entertained in the many Indian villages they passed through by the way.

They brought back early in the autumn, glowing accounts of the beauty of the region, and of the luxuriant meadows which bordered the stream. Governor Winthrop then sent a vessel on a trading voyage, through Long Island Sound, to Manhattan, there to inform the Dutch authorities that the king of England had granted the Connecticut river and the adjacent country to the subjects of Great Britain.

In most of these transactions the Dutch appear to great advantage. After five weeks' absence the vessel returned to Boston to report the friendly reception of the Massachusetts party at Manhattan, and bearing a courteous letter to Governor Winthrop, in which Van Twiller, in respectful terms, urged him to defer his claim to Connecticut until the king of England and the States-General of Holland should agree about their limits, so that the colonists of both nations, might live "as good neighbors in these heathenish countries." Director Van Twiller added, with good sense, which does him much credit :

"I have, in the name of the States-General and the West India Company, taken possession of the forementioned river, and, for testimony thereof, have set up an house on the north side of the said river.

It is not the intent of the States to take the land from the poor natives, but rather to take it at some reasonable price, which, God be praised, we have done hitherto.   In this part of the world there are many heathen lands which are destitute of inhabitants, so that there need not be any question respecting a little part or portion thereof."

At the same time the Plymouth colony made a move to obtain a foothold upon the Connecticut. To secure the color of a title, the colony purchased of a company of Indians who had been driven from their homes by the all-victorious Pequods, a tract of land just above fort Hope, embracing the territory where the town of Windsor now stands.   Lieutenant Holmes was then dispatched with a chosen company, in a vessel which conveyed the frame of a small house carefully stowed away, and which could be very expeditiously put together.   He was directed to push directly by fort Hope, and raise and fortify his house upon the purchased lands. Governor Bradford, of Plymouth, gives the following quaint account of this adventure:

"When they came up the river the Dutch demanded what they intended, and whither they would go?   They answered, 'up the river to trade.' Now their order was to go and seat above them. They bid them strike and stay or they would shoot them, and stood by their ordnance ready fitted. They answered, they had commission from the Governor of Plymouth to go up the river to such a place, and if they did shoot they must obey their order and proceed; they would not molest them but go on. So they passed along. And though the Dutch threatened them hard yet they shot not. Coming to their place they clapped up their house quickly, and landed their provisions, and left the company appointed, and sent the bark home, and afterward palisaded their house about, and fortified themselves better."

Van Twiller, informed of this intrusion, sent a commissioner, protesting against this conduct and ordering Holmes to depart, with all his people. Holmes replied, " I am here in the name of the king of England, and here I shall remain."

Matters soon became seriously complicated. A boat's crew was robbed and murdered by some vagabond Indians. The culprits were taken and hung.

This exasperated against the Dutch the powerful Pequods who had the supremacy over all that territory. Open war soon ensued. The Pequods sent an embassy to Boston, and entered into a treaty of alliance with the Massachusetts colony, in which they surrendered to that colony the Connecticut valley.

In the meantime, Van Twiller having received instructions from the home government, dispatched a force of seventy well armed men to drive Lieutenant Holmes and his men from their post. The English stood firmly upon their defence. The Dutch, seeing that a bloody battle must ensue, with uncertain results, withdrew without offering any violence. In many respects the Dutch colonies continued to enjoy much prosperity. Mr. Brodhead gives the following interesting account of the state of affairs at the mouth of the Hudson, in the year 1633 :

"Fort Amsterdam, which had become dilapidated, was repaired, and a guard-house and a barrack for the newly arrived soldiers were constructed within the ramparts, at a cost of several thousand guilders.

" Three expensive windmills were also erected. But they were injudiciously placed so near the fort that the buildings, within its walls, frequently intercepted and turned off the south wind.

" Several brick and frame houses were built for the Director and his officers. On the Company's farm, north of the fort, a dwelling-house, brewery, boat-house and barn were erected. Other smaller houses were built for the corporal, the smith, the cooper. The loft, in which the people had worshipped since 1626, was now replaced by a plain

wooden building, like a barn, situated on the East
River, in what is now Broad street, between Pearl
and Bridge streets.   Near this old church a dwelling-
house and stable were erected for the use of the
Domine.   In the Fatherland the title of Domine
was familiarly given to clergymen.   The phrase
crossed the Atlantic with Bogardus, and it has survived to the present day among the descendants of
the Dutch colonists of New Netherland."

The little settlement at Manhattan was entitled
to the feudal right of levying a tax upon all the
merchandise passing up or down the river.   The
English were, at this time, so ignorant of this region of the North American coast that a sloop was
dispatched to Delaware Bay "to see if there were
any river there."   As the Dutch had vacated the
Delaware, the English decided to attempt to obtain a foothold on those waters.   Accordingly, in
the year 1635, they sent a party of fourteen or
fifteen Englishmen, under George Holmes, to seize
the vacant Dutch fort.

Van Twiller, informed of this fact, with much
energy sent an armed vessel, by which the whole
company was arrested and brought to Manhattan,
whence they were sent, "pack and sack," to an
English settlement on the Chesapeake.

The Plymouth people had now been two years

in undisturbed possession of their post at Windsor, on the Connecticut.   Stimulated by their example, the General Court of Massachusetts encouraged emigration to the Connecticut valley, urging, as a consideration, their need of pasturage for their increasing flocks and herds ; the great beauty and fruitfulness of the Connecticut valley, and the danger that the Dutch, or other English colonies, might get possession of it.   "Like the banks of the Hudson," it was said, " the Connecticut had been first explored and even occupied by the Dutch.   But should a log hut and a few straggling soldiers seal a territory against other emigrants ? "*

Thus solicited, families from Watertown and Roxbury commenced a settlement at Wethersfield in the year 1635.   Some emigrants, from Dorchester, established themselves just below the colony of the Plymouth people at Windsor.   This led to a stern remonstrance on the part of Governor Bradford, of Plymouth, denouncing their unrighteous intrusion.   " Thus the Plymouth colonists on the Connecticut, themselves intruders within the territory of New Netherland, soon began to quarrel with their Massachusetts brethren for trespassing upon their usurped domain."

In November of this year, Governor Winthrop

* Hist. of New York, by John Romeyn Brodhead. Vol. I, p. 257.

dispatched a bark of twenty tons from Boston, with about twenty armed men, to take possession of the mouth of the Connecticut. It will be remembered that the Dutch had purchased this land of the Indians three years before, and, in token of their possession, had affixed the arms of the States-General to a tree. The English contemptuously tore down these arms, "and engraved a ridiculous face in their place."

The Dutch had called this region, Kievit's Hook. The English named it Saybrook, in honor of lords Say and Brook, who were regarded as the leading English proprietors. Early the next year the Massachusetts people established a colony at Agawam, now Springfield. Thus, step by step, the English encroached upon the Dutch, until nearly the whole valley of the Connecticut was wrested from them.

About this time Van Twiller issued a grant of sixty-two acres of land, a little northwest of fort Amsterdam, to Roelof Jansen. This was the original conveyance of the now almost priceless estate, held by the corporation of Trinity Church. The directors, in Holland, encouraged emigration by all the means in their power. Free passage was offered to farmers and their families. They were also promised the lease of a farm, fit for the plough, for six years, with a dwelling house, a barn, four horses and four cows. They were to pay a rent for these six years, of forty dollars a year, and eighty pounds of butter.

At the expiration of the six years the tenants were to restore the number of cattle they had received, retaining the increase. They were also assisted with clothing, provisions, etc., on credit, at an advance of fifty per cent. But notwithstanding the rapid increase of the Dutch settlements, thus secured, the English settlements were increasing with still greater rapidity. Not satisfied with their encroachments on the Connecticut, the English looked wistfully upon the fertile lands extending between that stream and the Hudson.

The region about New Haven, which, from the East and West rocks, was called the Red Rocks, attracted especial attention. Some men from Boston, who had visited it, greatly extolled the beauty and fertility of the region, declaring it to be far superior to Massachusetts Bay. "The Dutch will seize it," they wrote, "if we do not. And it is too good for any but friends."

Just then an English non-conformist clergyman, John Davenport, and two merchants from London, men of property and high religious worth, arrived at Boston. They sailed to the Red Rocks, purchased a large territory of the Indians, and regardless of the Dutch title, under the shadow of a great oak, laid the foundations of New Haven. The colony was very prosperous, and, in one year's time, numbered over one hundred souls.

And now the English made vigorous efforts to gain all the lands as far west as the Hudson river. A village of fifty log huts soon rose at Stratford, near the Housatonic. Enterprising emigrants also pushed forward as far as Norwalk, Stamford and Greenwich. The colony at Saybrook consisted in 1640, of a hundred houses, and a fine church. The Dutch now held, in the Connecticut valley, only the flat lands around fort Hope. And even these the English began to plough up. They cudgelled those of the Dutch garrison who opposed them, saying, "It would be a sin to leave uncultivated so valuable a land which can produce such excellent corn."

The English now laid claim to the whole of Long Island, and commenced a settlement at its eastern extremity. In the meantime very bitter complaints were sent to Holland respecting the incapacity of the Director Van Twiller. It was said that he, neglecting the affairs of the colony, was directing all his energies to enriching himself. He had become, it was reported, the richest landholder in the province. Though sustained by very powerful friends, he was removed.

William Kieft was appointed in his stead, the fifth Director. He was a man of very unenviable reputation, and his administration was far from successful. Mr. Brodhead gives the following true and very interesting account of the abundant natural resources of the Dutch settlements on the Hudson at this time:

" The colonists lived amid nature's richest profusion. In the forests, by the water side, and on the islands, grew a rank abundance of nuts and plums. The hills were covered with thickets of blackberries. On the flat lands, near the rivers, wild strawberries came up so plentifully that the people went there to lie down. and eat them. Vines, covered with grapes as good and sweet as in Holland, clambered over the loftiest trees. Deer abounded in the forests, in harvest time and autumn, as fat as any Holland deer can be. Enormous wild turkeys and myriads of partridges, pheasants and pigeons roosted in the neighboring woods. Sometimes the turkeys and deer came down to the houses of the colonists to feed. A stag was frequently sold by the Indians for a loaf of bread, or a knife, or even for a tobacco pipe. The river produced the finest fish. There was a great plenty of sturgeon, which, at that time,

the christians did not make use of, but the Indians
ate them greedily. Flax and hemp grew spontaneously. Peltries and hides were brought in great
quantities, by the savages, and sold for trifles. The
land was very well provisioned with all the necessaries of life."*

Thus far, as a general rule, friendly relations had
existed between the Dutch and the Indians. But
all sorts of characters were now emigrating from the
old world. The Indians were often defrauded, or
treated harshly. Individuals among the natives
retaliated by stealing. When caught they were
severely punished. Notwithstanding the government prohibited the sale of muskets to the Indians,
so eager were the savages to gain these weapons, so
invaluable to them on their hunting-fields, that they
would offer almost any price for them. Thus the
Mohawks ere long obtained "guns, powder and
bullets for four hundred warriors."

Kieft endeavored to tax the Indians, extorting
payment in corn and furs. This exasperated them.
Their reply, through one of their chiefs, would have
done honor to any deliberative assembly. Indignantly the chief exclaimed:

"How can the sachem at the fort dare to exact
a tax from us! He must be a very shabby fellow.

* History of the State of New York, p. 203.

He has come to live in our land when we have not invited him; and now he attempts to deprive us of our corn for nothing. The soldiers at fort Amsterdam are no protection to us. Why should we be called upon to support them? We have allowed the Dutch to live peaceably in our country, and have never demanded of them any recompense. When they lost a ship here, and built a new one, we supplied them with food and all other necessaries. We took care of them for two winters until their ship was finished. The Dutch are under obligations to us. We have paid full price for everything we have purchased of them. There is, therefore, no reason why we should supply them with corn and furs for nothing. If we have ceded to them the country they are living in, we yet remain masters of what we have retained for ourselves."

This unanswerable argument covered the whole ground. The most illiterate Indian could feel the force of such logic.

Some European vagabonds, as it was afterwards clearly proved, stole some swine from Staten Island. The blame was thrown upon the innocent Raritan Indians, who lived twenty miles inland. The rash Director Kieft resolved to punish them with severity which should be a warning to all the Indians.

He sent to this innocent, unsuspecting tribe, a

party of seventy well armed men, many of them un-principled desperadoes. They fell upon the peace-ful Indians, brutally killed several, destroyed their crops, and perpetrated all sorts of outrages.

The Indians never forget a wrong. The spirit of revenge burned in their bosoms. There was a thriv-ing plantation belonging to DeVrees on Staten Isl-and. The Indians attacked it, killed four of the laborers, burned the dwelling and destroyed the crops. Kieft, in his blind rage, resolved upon the extermination of the Raritans. He offered a large bounty for the head of any member of that tribe.

It will be remembered that some years before an Indian had been robbed and murdered near the pond, in the vicinity of the fort at Manhattan, and that his nephew, a boy, had escaped. That boy was now a man, and, through all these years, with almost religious scrupulousness, had been cherishing his sense of duty to avenge his uncle's unatoned death.

A very harmless Dutchman, by the name of Claes Smits, had reared his solitary hut upon the Indian trail near the East river. The nephew of the murdered savage came one day to this humble dwelling, and stopped under the pretence of selling some beaver skins. As Smits was stooping over the great chest in which he kept his goods, the savage, seizing an axe, killed him by a single blow. In doing this, he probably felt the joys of an approving conscience,—a conscience all uninstructed in religious truth—and thanked the great spirit that he had at length been enabled to discharge his duty in avenging his uncle's death.

Kieft sent to the chief of the tribe, demanding the murderer. The culprit Indian sent back the reply:

"When the fort was building some years ago, my uncle and I, carrying some beaver skins to the fort to trade, were attacked by some Dutchmen, who killed my uncle and stole the furs. This happened when I was a small boy. I vowed to revenge it upon the Dutch when I grew up. I saw no better chance than this of Claes Smits."

The sachem refused to deliver up the criminal, saying that he had but done his duty, according to the custom of his race, in avenging the death of his kinsman, murdered many years before. Kieft was exceedingly embarrassed. He was very unpopular; was getting the colony deeper and deeper into difficulty, and was accused of seeking war with the Indians that he "might make a wrong reckoning with the Company."

In this emergency, that others might share the responsibility with him, he reluctantly sought the counsel of the community. Twelve "select men"

5

were chosen to consider the propositions to be submitted to them by the Director.   To them the question was propounded:

"Is it not just, that the murder lately committed
by a savage, upon Claes Smits, be avenged and punished?   In case the Indians will not surrender the
murderer, is it not just to destroy the whole village
to which he belongs?   In what manner, when, and
by whom ought this to be executed?"

The result of their deliberations was, in brief, as
follows: "Our harvest is still ungathered; our cattle are scattered in the woods.   Many of the inhabitants, unsuspicious of danger, are at a distance.   It
is not best to precipitate hostilities.   In the meantime let two hundred coats of mail be procured in
preparation for the expedition..   Let our friendly intercourse with the savages be uninterrupted, to
throw them off their guard.   When the hunting season commences, let two armed bands be sent out to
attack the Indians from opposite directions.   Let as
many negroes as can be spared, be sent on this expedition, each armed with tomahawk and half-pike.
Still let messengers be sent once, twice and even a
third time to solicit the surrender of the murderer."

The Governor had the reputation of being an
arrant coward.   It had often been said, "It is very
well for him to send us into the field, while he se-

cures his own life in a good fort, out of which he
has not slept a single night in all the years he has
been here." They therefore shrewdly added, "The
Governor himself ought to lead the van in this attack. We will follow his steps and obey his com-
mands."

The hunting season soon came. Still it was decided to delay hostilities. The savages were on
their guard. A very general feeling of unfriendli-
ness pervaded the tribes. The Dutch settlers were
widely scattered. A combination of the Indians
against the colonists might prove an awful calamity.
Thus, for a time, the war which was evidently approaching was averted.

CHAPTER V.

War and Its Devastations.

Approaching Hostilities.—Noble Remonstrance.—Massacre of the Natives.—The War Storm.—Noble conduct of DeVrees.—The Humiliation of Kieft.—Wide-Spread Desolation.—The Reign of Terror.—State of Affairs at Fort Nassau.—The Massacre at Stamford.—Memorial of the Select Men.—Kieft Superseded by Peter Stuyvesant.

THE year 1643 was a year of terror and of blood in nearly all of the American colonies. New England was filled with alarm in the apprehension of a general rising of the Indians. It was said that a benighted traveller could not halloo in the woods without causing fear that the savages were torturing their European captives. This universal panic pervaded the Dutch settlements. The wildest stories were circulated at the firesides of the lonely settlers. Anxiety and terror pervaded all the defenceless hamlets.

DeVrees, rambling one day with his gun upon his shoulder, met an Indian "who was very drunk." Coming up to the patroon, the Indian patted him upon the shoulder, in token of friendship, saying,

"You are a good chief. When we come to see

you, you give us milk to drink. I have just come from Hackensack where they sold me brandy, and then stole my beaver skin coat. I will take a bloody revenge. I will go home for my bow and arrows, and shoot one of those rascally Dutchmen who have stolen my coat."

DeVrees endeavored in vain to soothe him. He had hardly reached his home ere he heard that the savage had kept his vow. He had shot and killed an innocent man, one Garret Van Voorst, who was thatching the roof of a house. The chiefs of the tribe were terror-stricken, through fear of the white man's vengeance. They did not dare to go to the fort lest they should be arrested and held as, hostages. But they hastened to an interview with DeVrees, in whom they had confidence, and express-ed a readiness to make atonement for the crime, in accordance with the custom of their tribe, by paying a large sum to the widow of the murdered man.

It is worthy of notice that this custom, so uni-versal among the Indians, of a blood atonement of money, was also the usage of the tribes of Greece. We read in Homer's Iliad, as translated by Pope

" If a brother bleed,
On just atonement we remit the deed ;
A sire the slaughter of his sons forgives,
The price of blood discharged, the murderer lives."

At length, encouraged by DeVrees and accompanied by him, the chiefs ventured to fort Amsterdam. They explained to Kieft the occurrence, and proposed the expiatory offering to appease the widow's grief. Kieft was inexorable. Nothing but the blood of the criminal would satisfy him. In vain they represented that he was the son of a beloved chief, and that already he had fled far away to some distant tribe. Our sympathy for these men is strongly excited as we read their sorrowful yet noble remonstrance :

"Why," said they, "will you sell brandy to our young men? They are not used to it. It makes them crazy. Even your own people, who are accustomed to strong liquors, sometimes become drunk and fight with knives. Sell no more strong drink to the Indians, if you will avoid such mischief."

While this question was being agitated, the Mohawks from the upper part of the Hudson, came down in strong military bands, armed with muskets, upon the lower river tribes, attacked them with great ferocity, killed quite a number of their warriors, took the women and children captive, and destroyed their villages.

The lower river tribes all trembled before the terrible Iroquois. Large numbers of these subjugated tribes fled from the river banks, and from the region of Westchester, to Manhattan and to Pavonia, where Jersey City now stands. Here, stripped and panic-stricken, they encamped, "full a thousand strong."

The humane and judicious patroon, DeVrees, in whom the Indians seem to have reposed great confidence, had a beautiful estate several miles up the river, at a place called Vreesendael. It was a delightful spot of about five hundred fertile acres, through which wound a fine stream affording handsome mill seats. The meadows yielded hay enough spontaneously for two hundred head of cattle.

DeVrees, finding his house full of fugitive savages, on their retreat to Pavonia, at the mouth of the river, paddled down in a canoe through the floating ice to fort Amsterdam, to confer with Director Kieft upon the emergency. He urged upon the Director that these poor Indians, thus escaping from the terrible Iroquois and grateful for the protection which the Dutch had not denied them, might easily be won to a sincere friendship. On the other hand, some of the more fiery spirits in the colony thought that the occasion furnished them with an opportunity so to cripple the Indians as to render them forever after powerless. They sent in a petition to Kieft, saying,

"We entreat that immediate hostile measures may be directed against the savages. They have not yet delivered up the assassins of Smits and Van Voorst, and thus these murders remain unavenged. The national character of the Dutch must suffer. God has now delivered our enemies into our hands. Let us attack them. We offer our services, and urge that united parties of soldiers and civilians assail them at several points."

These views were in entire harmony with the wishes of the sanguinary Kieft. He was delighted with the prospect of a war in which victory seemed easy and certain. Disregarding the remonstrances of DeVrees, and of the christian minister Bogardus, he made efficient preparation for the slaughter of the helpless savages.

He sent his secretary and a military officer across the river to reconnoitre the position of the Indians. There were two bands of these trembling fugitives, one at Pavonia, on the Jersey side of the river, and one at Corlaer's Hook, on the Island of Manhattan, just above fort Amsterdam. Secretly, at midnight of the 25th of February, 1643, the armed bands advanced against their unsuspecting victims. They were sleeping in fancied security when the murderous assault commenced.

"The noise of muskets," writes Brodhead, " min-

gled with the shrieks of the terrified Indians. Neither age nor sex were spared. Warrior and squaw,
sachem and child, mother and babe, were alike massacred. Daybreak scarcely ended the furious slaughter. Mangled victims, seeking safety in the thickets,
were driven into the river. Parents, rushing to save
their children whom the soldiers had thrown into
the stream, were driven back into the waters and
drowned before the eyes of their unrelenting murderers."

" I sat up that night," writes DeVrees, " by the
kitchen fire at the Director's. About midnight,
hearing loud shrieks, I ran up to the ramparts of the
fort. Looking towards Pavonia, I saw nothing but
shooting, and heard nothing but the shrieks of Indians murdered in their sleep."

With the dawn of the morning the victorious
Dutch returned from their scene of slaughter, bearing with them about thirty prisoners, and the *heads*
instead of the *scalps* of many warriors. Kieft wel-
comed these blood-stained men with " shaking of
hands and congratulations." The tidings of this
outrage spread far and wide among the Indian
tribes in the valley of the Hudson and on the Long
Island shore.

Private enterprise, relying upon the protection
of Kieft, had sent out a foraging expedition upon

5*

Long Island. Kieft assumed that he saw signs
of hostility there. The unsuspecting savages were
plundered of two wagon loads of grain. These
Indians, who had thus far been the warmest friends
of the Dutch, were now justly roused to the highest
pitch of indignation. They immediately made common cause with the river tribes, who were almost
frenzied with the desire to avenge the midnight
massacres of Pavonia and Manhattan. The storm
which thus burst upon New Netherland was sudden
and awful. The savages, in their rage, developed
energy and power totally unanticipated.

Eleven tribes combined in the most furious
and merciless attacks upon the lonely farm-houses.
Everywhere the war-whoop resounded, and the
plumed and painted savages emerged from swamps
and thickets, and assailed every unprotected dwelling. The farmer was shot in the field, his dwelling
burned, and his wife and children were thrown into
the flames. Many women and children, their lives
being spared, were carried into captivity worse than
death. Houses, haystacks and granaries were fired.
Cattle were slain or driven off, and crops destroyed.

Terror held high carnival. From the banks of
the Raritan to the valley of the Housatonic, over a
region of hundreds of square miles, not a plantation
was safe. Men, women and children, haggard with

hunger, exposure and woe, fled from their deserted homes to fort Amsterdam. Despairing of ever again finding peaceful residence in this new world, with one voice they demanded a return to the fatherland. The Dutch colonies were threatened with immediate and entire depopulation.

Kieft himself was terrified in view of the frightful storm he had raised. He was compelled to enlist every able-bodied man as a soldier. There was an end to all traffic, to all agriculture, to all the arts of industry. Even the plantation of the humane De-Vrees did not escape the undiscriminating wrath of the savages. The outhouses, cattle and crops were utterly destroyed. Quite a number of the terrified colonists had taken refuge in the manor house which DeVrees had prudently built very strong, and constructed with loopholes for musketry.

The Indians were besieging the place, when one of their tribe came, whom DeVrees had assisted to escape from the massacre at Manhattan. He told the story of his escape and said that DeVrees was a good chief whom they ought to respect. The Indians held a short consultation, and then the grateful savages deputed one of their number to advance within speaking distance of the manor house. This man, whom we call a savage, cried out:

"We are very sorry that we have destroyed the outhouses, the cattle and the crops. We now know that chief DeVrees is a good chief and our friend. If we had not destroyed his property we would not do so. We will not harm the brewery, though we all greatly need the copper kettle to make barbs for our arrows."

These noble red men, for we must think they exhibited a noble spirit, then departed. DeVrees was, at the time, in the manor house. He hastened down the river to fort Amsterdam and indignantly addressing the governor, said:

"Has it not happened just as I foretold, that you are only helping to shed christian blood? Who will now compensate us for our losses?"

The wretched Kieft had not one word to reply. He however, made a weak and unavailing attempt to appease the wrath of the Long Island Indians. But the roaring tornado of savage vengeance could not thus be divested of its terrors. The messengers he sent, approaching a band of Indians, cried out to them, "We come to you as friends." They shouted back contemptuously, "Are you our friends? You are only corn thieves." Refusing all intercourse they disappeared in the forest.

During all these scenes the infamous and cowardly Kieft ensconced himself securely within the walls of the fort. The bewailings of ruined farmers, and of widows and orphan children rose all around him. To divert public clamor, he fitted out several expeditions against the Indians. But these expeditions all returned having accomplished nothing.

"The proud heart of the Director," writes Brodhead, "began to fail him at last. In one week desolation and sorrow had taken the place of gladness and prosperity. The colony entrusted to his charge was nearly ruined. It was time to humble himself before the Most High, and invoke from heaven the mercy which the christian had refused the savage.

"A day of general fasting and prayer was proclaimed. 'We continue to suffer much trouble and loss from the heathen, and many of our inhabitants see their lives and property in jeopardy, which is doubtless owing to our sins,' was Kieft's contrite confession, as he exhorted every one penitently to supplicate the mercy of God, 'so that his holy name may not, through our iniquities, be blasphemed by the heathen.' "

The people still held the Director responsible for all the consequences which had followed the massacres of Pavonia and Corlaer's Hook. They boldly talked of arresting and deposing him, and of sending him, as a culprit, back to Holland. The Director, panic-stricken, endeavored to shift the responsibility of the insane course which had been pursued, upon one Adriansen, an influential burgher, who was the leading man among the petitioners who had counselled war.

Adriansen was now a ruined man. His own plantation had been utterly devastated. Exasperated by his losses, he had no disposition to take upon himself the burden of that popular odium which had now become so heavy. Losing all self-control, he seized a sword and a pistol, and rushed into the Director's room, with the apparent intention of assassinating him, exclaiming, "what lies are these you are reporting of me."

He was disarmed and imprisoned. One of his servants took a gun, went to the fort and deliberately discharged the piece at the Director, but without hitting him. The would-be assassin was shot down by a sentinel and his' head exposed upon the scaffold. Adriansen was sent to Holland for trial.

After terrible scenes of suffering, a temporary peace was restored through the heroic interposition of DeVrees. He was the only man who dared to venture among the exasperated Indians. They watched over him kindly, and entreated him to be cautious in exposing himself, lest harm might befall him from some wandering Indians by whom he was not known. But the wrongs which the Indians had experienced were too deep to be buried in oblivion. And there was nothing in the character of Kieft to secure their confidence. After the truce of a few weeks the war, without any imaginable cause, broke out anew.

All the settlements at Westchester and Long Island were laid waste. Scarcely an inhabitant, save the roving Indian, was to be found in those regions. The Dutch were driven out of the whole of New Jersey. The settlers on Staten Island were trembling in hourly expectation of an assault. War's devastating surges of flame and blood swept nearly the whole island of Manhattan. Bold men ventured to remain well armed, upon a few of the farms, or *boweries* as they were called, in the immediate vicinity of the fort, but they were continually menaced with attack, night and day. A *bowery* was a farm on which the family resided. A plantation was one of those extended tracts of land, which was partly cultivated but upon which no settler dwelt. There was no protection anywhere for the trembling population, save in and directly around fort Amsterdam. Mr. Brodhead, alluding to these scenes of terror, writes,

"The women and children lay concealed in straw huts, while their husbands and fathers mounted guard on the crumbling ramparts above. For the fort itself was almost defenceless. It resembled rather a mole-hill than a fortress against an enemy. The cattle, which had escaped destruction, were huddled within the walls, and were already beginning to starve for want of forage. It was indispensable to maintain a constant guard at all hours, for seven allied tribes, well supplied with muskets, powder and ball, which they had procured from private traders, boldly threatened to attack the dilapidated citadel with all their strength, now amounting to fifteen hundred men.

"So confident had the enemy become, that their scouting parties constantly threatened the advanced sentinels of the garrison. Ensign Van Dyck, while relieving guard at one of the outposts, was wounded by a musket ball in his arm. All the forces that the Dutch could now muster, besides the fifty or sixty soldiers in garrison, were about two hundred freemen. With this handful of men was New Netherland to be defended against the implacable fury of her savage foe."

For a time the war which had desolated the region of the lower valley of the Hudson, did not reach fort Nassau, now Albany. The tribes resident there were at war with the lower river tribes. As these Indians still maintained apparently friendly relations with the whites, the patroon, Van Rensselaer, allowed his agents freely to sell to them fire-arms and powder.

This distant and feeble post at this time consisted only of a wretched little fort built of logs, with eight or ten small cannon or swivels.

A hamlet of about thirty huts was scattered along the river. A church, thirty-four feet long by nineteen wide, had been erected in a pine grove within range of the guns of the fort. Nine benches accommodated the congregation. A very faithful pastor, Domine Megapolensis, ministered to them.

The red men were often attracted to the church to hear the preached gospel, and wondered what it meant. Megapolensis writes :

"When we have a sermon sometimes ten or twelve of the Indians will attend, each having in his mouth a long tobacco pipe made by himself, and will stand awhile and look. Afterwards they will ask me what I was doing, and what I wanted, that I stood there alone and made so many words and none of the rest might speak.

"I tell them that I admonish the christians that they must not steal or drink, or commit murder, or do anything wrong, and that I intend, after a while, to come and preach to them when I am acquainted with their language. They say that I do well in teaching the christians, but immediately add, 'Why do so many christians do these things?'"

This was several years before John Eliot commenced preaching the gospel to the Indians near Boston. Kieft very earnestly applied to the English colony at New Haven for assistance against the Indians. The proposal was submitted to the General Court. After mature deliberation, it was decided that the Articles of Confederation between the New England colonies prohibited them from engaging separately in war; and that moreover "they were not satisfied that the Dutch war with the Indians was just."

The Dutch Director, thus disappointed in obtaining assistance from the English, was roused to the energies of desperation. The spirit of the people also rose to meet the emergency. It was determined to commence the most vigorous offensive measures against the savages.

We have not space to enter into the details of this dreadful war. We will record one of its sanguinary scenes, as illustrative of many others. The Connecticut Indians, in the vicinity of Greenwich, had joined the allied tribes, and were becoming increasingly active in their hostility. Ensign Van Dyck was dispatched with one hundred and fifty men in three vessels. The expedition landed at

Greenwich. The Indian warriors, over five hundred in number, were assembled in a strongly palisaded village in the vicinity of Stamford.

It was midnight in February, 1644, when the expedition approached the Indian village. All the day long the men had toiled through the snow. It was a wintry night, clear and cold, with a full moon whose rays, reflected by the dazzling surface of hill and valley, were so brilliant that "many winter days were not brighter."

The Dutch, discharging a volley of bullets upon the doomed village, charged, sword in hand. The savages, emboldened by their superior numbers, made a desperate resistance. But in a conflict like this, arrows are comparatively powerless when opposed to muskets. The Indians, unable to reach their foes with their arrows, made several very bold sallies, recklessly endeavoring to break the Dutch lines. They were invariably driven back with great loss. Not one of them could show himself outside the palisades without being shot down.

In less than an hour the dark forms of one hundred and eighty Indian warriors lay spread out upon the blood-crimsoned snow. And now the Dutch succeeded in applying the torch. The whole village, composed of the most combustible materials, was instantly in flames. The Indians lost all self-posses-

sion. They ran to and fro in a state of frenzy. As
they endeavored to escape they were, with unerring
aim, shot down, or driven back into their blazing
huts. Thus over five hundred perished. Of all who
crowded the little village at nightfall but eight
escaped. Only eight of the Dutch were wounded;
but not one fatally.

The conflagration of an hour laid the bark village
in ashes. Nothing remained. The victors built
large fires and bivouacked upon the snow. The
next day they returned to Stamford, and two days
afterward reached fort Amsterdam.

War is generally ruin to both parties. In this
case neither of the combatants gained anything.
Both parties alike reaped but a harvest of blood and
woe. Scouting parties of the savages prowled
beneath the very walls of fort Amsterdam, ready at
a moment's warning, to dart into the wilderness,
where even the bravest of the Dutch could not venture to pursue. For the protection of the few cattle
which remained, all the men turned out and built a
stout fence, "from the great bowery or farm across
to Emanuel plantation," near the site of the present
Wall street.

During the whole summer of 1644, the savages
were busy carrying the desolating war into every
unprotected nook and corner. The condition of

the colony became desperate, being almost entirely destitute of food, money and clothing. The utter incompetency of Kieft was daily more conspicuous. He did nothing. " Scarce a foot was moved on land, or an oar laid in the water." The savages, thus left in security to fish and gather in their crops, were ever increasingly insolent and defiant. One of the annalists of those times writes :

" Parties of Indians roved about day and night, over Manhattan island, killing the Dutch not a thousand paces from fort Amsterdam. No one dared to move a foot to fetch a stick of firewood without a strong escort."

Kieft, in his overwhelming embarrassments, had found it necessary to convene eight select men to advise him and to aid in supporting his authority. These select men decided to demand of the home government the recall of Kieft, whose incapacity had thus plunged the once-flourishing colony into utter ruin. They also urged the introduction into New Netherland of the municipal system of the fatherland.

In their brief but touching memorial they write, " Our fields lie fallow and waste. Our dwellings are burned. Not a handful can be sown this autumn on the deserted places. The crops, which God permitted to come forth during the summer, remain rotting

in the fields. We have no means to provide necessaries for wives or children. We sit here amidst
thousands of savages from whom we can find neither
peace nor mercy.

"There are those among us who, by the sweat
and labor of their hands, through many long years
and at great expense, have endeavored to improve
their land. Others have come with ships freighted
with a large quantity of cattle. They have cleared
away the forest, enclosed their plantations, and
brought them under the plough, so as to be an ornament to the country and a profit to the proprietors after their long and laborious toil. The whole
of these now lie in ashes through a foolish hanker-
ing after war.

"All right-thinking men here know that these
Indians have lived as lambs among us until a few
years ago, injuring no man, offering every assistance
to our nation, and when no supplies were sent for
several months, furnishing provisions to the Company's servants until they received supplies. These
hath the Director, by several uncalled-for proceedings
from time to time, so estranged from us, and so
embittered against the Netherlands nation, that we
do not believe that anything will bring them and
peace back, unless the Lord, who bends all hearts to
his will, propitiate their people.

"Little or nothing of any account has been done here for the country. Every place is going to ruin. Neither counsel nor advice is taken."

After giving an account of the origin and progress of the war, they warn the home government against relying upon the statements which the Director had sent over to them. "These statements," they said, "contain as many lies as lines." The memorial was concluded with the following forcible words:

"Honored Lords; this is what we have, in the sorrow of our hearts, to complain of. We shall end here, and commit the matter wholly to our God, praying that he will move your lordships' minds, so that a Governor may be speedily sent to us with a beloved peace, or that we may be permitted to return with our wives and children, to our dear fatherland. For it is impossible ever to settle this country until a different system be introduced here, and a new Governor sent out."

In response to this appeal Kieft was recalled. Just before he received his summons peace was concluded with the Indians, on the 31st of August, 1645. The war had raged five years. It had filled the land with misery. All were alike weary of its carnage and woes. A new governor was appointed, Peter Stuyvesant. The preceding account of the origin of the Dutch colony and its progress thus far is essential to the understanding of the long and successful administration of the new governor, whose name is one of the most illustrious in the early annals of New York.

It may be worthy of brief remark that a few weeks after the arrival of Governor Stuyvesant, Kieft embarked in the ship Princess for Holland. The vessel was wrecked on the coast of Wales. Kieft and eighty-one men, women and children sank into a watery grave. Kieft died unlamented. His death was generally regarded as an act of retributive justice.

CHAPTER VI.

Governor Stuyvesant.

New Netherland in 1646.—Early Years of Peter Stuyvesant.—Decay
of New Amsterdam.—The Germs of a Representative Government.—Energetic Administration.—Death of Governor Winthrop.—Claims for Long Island.—Arrogance of the Governor.—
Remonstrance of the Nine Men.—The Pastoral Office.—Boundary lines.—Increasing Discontent.—Division of Parties.—Dictatorial Measures.

IT is estimated that the whole population of New
Netherland, in the year 1646, amounted to about one
thousand souls. In 1643, it numbered three thousand. Such was the ruin which the mal-administra-
tion of Kieft had brought upon the colony. The
male adult population around Amsterdam was reduced to one hundred. At the same time the population of the flourishing New England colonies had
increased to about sixty thousand.

On the 11th of May, 1647, Governor Stuyvesant
arrived at Manhattan. He was appointed as " Re-
dresser General," of all colonial abuses. We have
but little knowledge of the early life of Peter Stuyvesant. The West India Company had a colony

upon the island of Curaçoa, in the Caribbean Sea. For some time Stuyvesant had been its efficient Director. He was the son of a clergyman in Friesland, one of the northern provinces of the Netherlands.

He received a good academic education, becoming quite a proficient in the Latin language, of which accomplishment, it is said that he was afterwards somewhat vain. At school he was impetuous, turbulent and self-willed. Upon leaving the academy he entered the military service, and soon developed such energy of character, such a spirit of self-reliance and such administrative ability that he was appointed director of the colony at Curaçoa. He was recklessly courageous, and was deemed somewhat unscrupulous in his absolutism. In an attack upon the Portuguese island of Saint Martin, in the year 1644, which attack was not deemed fully justifiable, he lost a leg. The wound rendered it necessary for him to return to Holland in the autumn of 1644, for surgical aid.

Upon his health being re-established, the Directors of the West India Company, expressing much admiration for his Roman courage, appointed him Governor of their colony in New Netherland, which was then in a state of ruin. There were also under his sway the islands of Curaçoa, Buenaire and

Amba. The Provincial Government presented him with a paper of instructions very carefully drawn up. The one-man power, which Kieft had exercised, was very considerably modified. Two prominent officers, the Vice-Director and the Fiscal, were associated with him in the administration of all civil and military affairs. They were enjoined to take especial care that the English should not further encroach upon the Company's territory. They were also directed to do everything in their power to pacify the Indians and to restore friendly relations with them. No fire-arms or ammunition were, under any circumstances, to be sold to the Indians.

Van Diricklagen was associated with the Governor as Vice-Director, and ensign Van Dyck, of whom the reader has before heard, was appointed Fiscal, an important office corresponding with our post of Treasurer. Quite a large number of emigrants, with abundant supplies, accompanied this party. The little fleet of four ships left the Texel on Christmas day of 1646. The expedition, running in a southerly direction, first visited the West India islands. On the voyage the imperious temper of Stuyvesant very emphatically developed itself.

Holland was then at war with Spain. A prize was captured and the question arose respecting its disposal. Fiscal Van Dyck claimed, by virtue of his office, a seat at the council board and a voice in the decision. The governor rudely repulsed him with the words,

"Get out. Who admitted you into the council. When I want you I will call you."

When they arrived at Curaçoa, Van Dyck again made an attempt to gain that place in the Council to which he thought his office legitimately entitled him. Stuyvesant punished him by confining him to the ship, not allowing him to step on shore. All the other officers and soldiers were freely allowed to recruit themselves by strolling upon the land.

Upon reaching Manhattan, Stuyvesant was received by the whole community with great rejoicing. And when he said, "I shall reign over you as a father governs his children," they were perhaps not fully aware of the dictatorial spirit which was to animate his government. With wonderful energy he immediately devoted himself to the reform of abuses. Though he availed himself of absolute power, taking counsel of no one, all his measures seem to have been adopted, not for the advancement of his own selfish interests, but for the promotion of the public good.

Proclamations were issued against Sabbath desecration, intemperance and all quarrelling. No intoxicating liquors were to be sold to the savages under a penalty of five hundred guilders. *And the seller was also to be held responsible for any injury which the savage might inflict, while under the influence of strong drink.* After the ringing of the nine o'clock bell in the evening, intoxicating drinks were not to be sold to any person whatever.

To draw a knife in a quarrel was to be punished with a heavy fine and six months imprisonment. If a wound was inflicted the penalty was trebled. Great faults accompanied this development of energy. The new governor assumed "state and pomp like a peacock's." He kept all at a distance from him, exacted profound homage, and led many to think that he would prove a very austere father. All his acts were characterized by great vigor.

New Amsterdam, at that time, presented a very dilapidated and deplorable appearance. The fort was crumbling to ruins. The skeleton of an unfinished church deformed the view. The straggling fences were broken down. The streets were narrow and crooked, many of the houses encroaching upon them. The foul enclosures for swine bordered the thoroughfares.

A system of taxation upon both exports and imports was introduced, which speedily replenished the treasury. Governor Stuyvesant was a professing

christian, being a devout member of the Reformed
Church of the fatherland.   He promptly transferred
his relations to the church at fort Amsterdam.   He
became an elder in the church, and conscious that
the christian religion was the basis of all prosperity,
one of his first acts was the adoption of measures
for the completion of the church edifice.   Proprietors
of vacant lots were ordered to fence them in and
improve them.   Surveyors of buildings were appointed to regulate the location and structure of new
houses.

The embarrassments which surrounded the governor were so great that he found it necessary to
support his authority by calling public opinion to
his aid.   "Necessity," writes Brodhead, "produced
concession and prerogative yielded to popular rights
The Council recommended that the principle of
representation should be conceded to the people.
Stuyvesant consented."

An election was ordered and eighteen "of the
most notable, reasonable, honest and respectable
persons" in the colony were chosen, from whom the
governor was to select nine persons as a sort of
privy council.   It is said that Stuyvesant was very
reluctant to yield at all to the people, and that he
very jealously guarded the concessions to which he
was constrained to assent.   By this measure popular

rights gained largely. The *Nine Men* had however only the power to give advice when it was asked. When assembled, the governor could attend the meeting and act as president.

Governor Stuyvesant, soon after his arrival at fort Amsterdam, addressed courteous letters to the governors of all the neighboring colonies. In his letter to Governor Winthrop, of Massachusetts, he asserted the indubitable right of the Dutch to all the territory between the Connecticut and the Delaware, and proposed an interview for the settlement of all difficulties.

An Amsterdam ship, the Saint Benino, entered the harbor of New Haven, and for a month engaged in trade without a license from the West India Company. Stuyvesant, ascertaining the fact, sent a company of soldiers on a secret expedition to New Haven, seized the vessel on the Lord's day, brought her to Manhattan, and confiscated both ship and cargo.

Emboldened by success, Stuyvesant sent a letter to the authorities at New Haven claiming all the region from Cape Henlopen to Cape Cod as part of the territory of New Netherland, and affirming his right to levy duties upon all Dutch vessels trading within those limits.

Governor Eaton, of the New Haven colony, sent

back a remonstrance protesting against the Dutch governor as a disturber of the public peace by "making unjust claims to our lands and plantations, to our havens and rivers, and by taking a ship out of our harbor without our license."

Three deserters from Manhattan fled to New Haven. Governor Eaton, though bound by treaty obligations to deliver them up, yet indignant in view of what he deemed the arrogant claim of Governor Stuyvesant, refused to surrender them, lest the surrender should be deemed as " done in the way of subordination." The impetuous Stuyvesant at once issued a retaliatory proclamation in which he said:

" If any person, noble or ignoble, freeman or slave, debtor or creditor, yea, to the lowest prisoner included, run away from the colony at New Haven, or seek refuge in our limits, he shall remain free, under our protection, on taking the oath of allegiance."

This decree excited strong disapprobation at home as well as in the other colonies. The inhabitants of Manhattan objected to it as tending to convert the province into a refuge for vagabonds from the neighboring English settlements. After a few months the obnoxious proclamation was revoked. But in the meantime Governor Stuyvesant had brib d the runaways, who had been taken into the public service at New Haven, to escape and return home.

As a precaution against fire, it was ordered that if a house were burned through the owner's negligence, he should be heavily fined. Fire-wardens were appointed to inspect the buildings. If any chimney was found foul, the owner was fined and the sum was appointed to purchasing fire-ladders, hooks and buckets. As nearly one-fourth of the houses were licensed for the sale of brandy, tobacco or beer, it was resolved that no farther licenses should be granted. It was ordered that cattle and swine should be pastured within proper enclosures. And it was also ordained that, "from this time forth, in the afternoon as well as in the forenoon, there shall be preaching from God's word." Many of the Indians were employed as servants or day laborers. They were often defrauded of their wages. A decree was issued, punishing with a fine those who neglected to pay these debts.

In January, 1649, Charles I., of England, was beheaded in front of his own banqueting hall, and England became nominally a republic. The event created the most profound sensation throughout all christendom. The shock, which agitated all Europe, was felt in America. The prince of Wales and the duke of York, escaping from England, took refuge

6*

in Holland with their brother-in-law, the stadtholder, William, prince of Orange. A rupture between England and Holland appeared imminent. The Puritans in America were well pleased with the establishment of a republic in their native land. A war between the two European nations would probably bring all the Dutch colonies under the control of England. The West India Company, in view of these perils, urged Stuyvesant "to live with his neighbors on the best terms possible."

On the 24th of March, of this year, the venerable Governor Winthrop, of Massachusetts, died, at the age of sixty-one. Governor Eaton, of New Haven, proposed to Stuyvesant a meeting of the Governors, at Boston, to discuss the affairs of the colonies. The meeting was held in August. It was not harmonious. The Dutch were forbidden from trading anywhere with the Indians within the territory of the English colonies, and Stuyvesant was very emphatically informed that the English claimed all the territory between Cape Cod and New Haven.

Lady Stirling, widow of Lord Stirling, determined to maintain her title to the whole of Long Island. She sent an agent, who announced himself to the English settlers at Hempstead, on the northern portion of the island, as governor of the whole island under the Dowager Countess of Stirling. Intelligence of this was speedily sent to Stuyvesant. The Dutch Governor caused his immediate arrest, ordered him, notwithstanding his "very consequential airs," to be examined before the council, took copies of his papers, and placed him on board ship for Holland. The ship put in at an English port, the agent escaped and was heard of no more.

The council, much displeased with the absolutism assumed by Stuyvesant, resolved to send one of their number, a remarkably energetic man, Adrien Van Der Donck, to Holland to seek redress from the home government. The movement was somewhat secret, and they endeavored to conceal from the governor the papers which were drawn up, containing the charges against him. The spirit of Stuyvesant was roused.

He went in person, with some officers, to the chamber of Van Der Donck, when he was absent, seized his papers, and then caused him to be arrested and imprisoned.

The Vice Director, Van Diricklagen, accompanied by a delegation from the people, protested against these proceedings, and demanded that Van Der Donck should be released from captivity and held on bail. Stuyvesant refused, saying that the prisoner was arrested, " for calumniating the officers of government; that his conduct tended to bring the sovereign authority into contempt." Van Der Donck was punished by banishment from the council and from the board of Nine Men.

Just before this, two prominent men, Kuyter and Melyn, demanded an appeal to the people in reference to some act of Kieft's reckless administration. Stuyvesant took the alarm. If the people could judge of Kieft's administration, his own might be exposed to the same ordeal. Convening a special council, he said,

" These petitioners are disturbers of the public peace. If we grant their request, will not the cunning fellows, in order to usurp over us a more unlimited power, claim even greater authority against ourselves, should it happen that our administration may not square in every respect with their whims. It is treason to petition against one's magistrate whether there be cause or not."

The unfortunate petitioners were now arraigned on various charges. The Governor and his subservient Council acted both as prosecutors and judges. The prisoners were accused of instigating the war with the savages, of counselling the mortgaging of Manhattan to the English, and of threatening Kieft with personal violence. The case was speedily decided and sentence was pronounced. Stuyvesant

wished Melyn to be punished with death and confiscation of property. But the majority of the Council
held back the Governor's avenging hand. Still he
succeeded in sentencing Melyn to seven years' banishment, to a fine of three hundred guilders, and to
forfeit all benefits derived from the Company. Kuyter was sentenced to three years' banishment and to
a fine of one hundred and fifty guilders. They were
also denied the right of appeal to the fatherland.

" If I were persuaded," said the Governor, " that
you would divulge our sentence, or bring it before
their High Mightinesses, I would have you hanged
at once, on the highest tree in New Netherland."

Again he said, with characteristic energy, " If any
one, during my administration, shall appeal, I will
make him a foot shorter, and send the pieces to
Holland and let him appeal in that way."*

Melyn and Kuyter being sent to Holland as crim-
inals, did appeal to the home government; their
harsh sentence was suspended; they were restored
to all the rights of colonists of New Netherland, and
Stuyvesant was cited to defend his sentence at the
Hague. When Melyn returned to Manhattan with
these authoritative papers, a great tumult was excited. Anxious that his triumph should be as public

* History of the State of New York, By John Romeyn Brodhead Vol I. p. 473.

as his disgrace had been, he demanded that the
Acts should be read to the people assembled in the
church. With much difficulty he carried his point.
"I honor the States and shall obey their com-
mands," said Stuyvesant, "I shall send an attorney
to sustain the sentence."

The Indians loudly, and with one accord, demanded the right to purchase fire-arms. For years
they had been constantly making such purchases,
either through the colonists at Rensselaerswyck, or
from private traders. It was feared that the persist-
ent refusal to continue the supply, might again instigate them to hostilities. The Directors of the
West India government therefore intimated that
"it was the best policy to furnish them with powder and ball, but with a sparing hand."

Stuyvesant ordered a case of guns to be brought
over from Holland. They were landed openly at
fort Amsterdam and placed under the care of an
agent of the governor. Thus Stuyvesant himself
was to monopolize the trade, which was extremely
lucrative; for the Indians would pay almost any
price for guns, powder and shot. This increased the
growing dissatisfaction. The Indians would readily
exchange skins to the amount of forty dollars for a
gun, and of four dollars for a pound of powder.

"The governor," it was said, "assumes to be

everything. He establishes shops for himself and does the business of the whole country. He is a brewer and has breweries. He is a ship-owner, a merchant, and a trader in both lawful and contraband articles."

The Nine Men persisted in their resolve to send a remonstrance to the fatherland. The memorial was signed and forwarded the latter part of July. In this important document, which first gave a brief account of the past history of the colony, the administration of Stuyvesant was reviewed with much severity.

"In our opinion," said the remonstrants, "this country will never flourish under the present government. The country must be provided with godly, honorable and intelligent rulers, who are not very indigent, and who are not too covetous. The mode in which this country is now governed is intolerable. Nobody is secure in his property longer than the Director pleases, who is generally strongly inclined to confiscating. A good population would be the consequence of a good government. Many would be allured here by the pleasantness, situation, salubrity and fruitfulness of the country, if protection were secured."

Three of the signers were deputed to convey the remonstrance to the Hague and lay it before the

authorities there.   The pastor of the church at Manhattan, Domine Backerus, returned to Holland with
the commissioners.   He was greatly dissatisfied with
the regime of the governor, and upon his arrival in
Holland, joined the complainants.

Domine Megapolensis, who had been pastor
of the church at Rensselaerswyck, having obtained
letters of dismission from his church, was also about
to sail to the fatherland.   The colonists, generally
religiously disposed, were greatly troubled, being
threatened with a total loss of the gospel ministry.
By the earnest solicitation of Stuyvesant, he consented to remain at Manhattan, where he was
formally installed as pastor of the church, upon a
salary of twelve hundred guilders, which was about
four hundred dollars.   At the same time the energetic governor manifested his interest in education
by writing earnestly to Amsterdam, urging that a
pious, well-qualified and diligent schoolmaster might
be sent out.   " Nothing," he added, " is of greater
importance than the right, early instruction of
youth."

The governor was sorely annoyed by the action
of the States-General, reversing his sentence against
Melyn and Kuyter.   He wrote that he should obey
their decision, but that he would rather never have
received their commission as governor, than to have

had his authority lowered in the eyes of his neighbors and friends.

The three commissioners, bearing the memorial of the Nine Men, reached Holland in safety. The States-General received their memorial, and also listened to the reply of the agent, whom Stuyvesant had sent out to plead his cause. The decision of the States was virtually a rebuke of the dictatorial government of Stuyvesant, and several very important reforms were ordered. This decision displeased the West India Company. Those men deemed their rights infringed upon by this action of the States-General. They were therefore led to espouse the cause of the governor. Thus strengthened, Stuyvesant ventured to disregard the authority of the States-General.

The Dutch at Manhattan began to be clamorous for more of popular freedom. Stuyvesant, hoping to enlist the sympathies of the governors of the English colonies in his behalf, made vigorous arrangements for the long projected meeting with the Commissioners of the United Colonies.

On the 17th of September, 1650, Governor Stuyvesant embarked at Manhattan, with his secretary, George Baxter, and quite an imposing suite. Touching at several places along the sound, he arrived at Hartford in four days. After much discus-

sion it was agreed to refer all differences, of the
points in controversy, to four delegates, two to be
chosen from each side. It is worthy of special remark that Stuyvesant's secretary was an Englishman, and he chose two Englishmen for his delegates.

In the award delivered by the arbitrators, it was
decided that upon Long Island a line running from
the westernmost part of Oyster Bay, in a straight
direction to the sea, should be the bound between
the English and the Dutch territory; the easterly
part to belong to the English, the westernmost part
to the Dutch. Upon the mainland, the boundary
line was to commence on the west side of Greenwich
bay, about four miles from Stamford; and to run in
a northerly direction twenty miles into the country,
provided that the said line came not within ten
miles of the Hudson river. The Dutch were not to
build any house within six miles of said line. The
inhabitants of Greenwich were to remain, till further
consideration, under the Government of the Dutch.
It was also decided that a nearer union of friendship
and amity, between England and the Dutch colonies
in America, should be recommended to the several
jurisdictions of the United Colonies.

Stuyvesant reported the result of these negotiations to the Chamber at Amsterdam but, for some

unexplained reason, did not send to that body a copy of the treaty. Upon his return to Manhattan he was immediately met with a storm of discontent. His choice of two Englishmen as the referees, to represent the Dutch cause, gave great offence. It was deemed an insult to his own countrymen. There was a general disposition with the colonists to repudiate a treaty which the Dutch had had no hand in forming. Complaints were sent to Holland that the Governor had surrendered more territory than might have formed fifty colonies ; and that, rejecting those reforms in favor of popular rights which the home government had ordered, he was controlling all things with despotic power.

" This grievous and unsuitable government," the Nine Men wrote, "ought at once to be reformed. The measures ordered by the home government should be enforced so that we may live as happily as our neighbors. Our term of office is about to expire. The governor has declared that he will not appoint any other select men. ·We shall not dare again to assemble in a body ; for we dread unjustifiable prosecutions, and we can already discern the smart thereof from afar." *

Notwithstanding these reiterated rebukes, Stuy-

* John Romeyn Brodhead, Vol. I. p. 521. E. B. O'Callaghan. M. D. Vol 2. p. 157.

vesant persisted in his arbitrary course. The vice-
director, Van Diricklagen, and the fiscal or treasurer
Van Dyck, united in a new protest expressing the
popular griefs. Van Der Donck was the faithful
representative of the commonalty in their fatherland. The vice-director, in forwarding the new protest to him wrote,

"Our great Muscovy duke keeps on as of old;
something like the wolf, the longer he lives the
worse he bites."

It is a little remarkable that the English refugees, who were quite numerous in the colony, were
in sympathy with the arbitrary assumptions of the
governor. They greatly strengthened his hands by
sending a Memorial to the West India Company,
condemning the elective franchise which the Dutch
colonists desired.

"We willingly acknowledge," they wrote, "that
the power to elect a governor from among ourselves,
which is, we know, the design of some here, would
be our ruin, by reason of our factions and the difference of opinion which prevails among us."

The West India Company, not willing to relin-
quish the powers which it grasped, was also in very
decided opposition to the spirit of popular freedom
which the Dutch colonists were urging, and which
was adopted by the States-General. Thus, in this

great controversy, the governor, the West India Company and the English settlers in the colony were on one side. Upon the other side stood the States-General and the Dutch colonists almost without exception.

The vice-director was punished for his protest, by expulsion from the council and by imprisonment in the guard-room for four days. Upon his liberation he took refuge with the Patroon on Staten Island. The notary, who had authenticated the protest, was dismissed from office and forbidden any farther to practice his profession. In every possible way, Stuyvesant manifested his displeasure against his own countrymen of the popular party, while the English were treated with the utmost consideration.

In the treaty of Hartford no reference was made to the interests of the Dutch on the south, or Delaware river. The New Haven people equipped a vessel and dispatched fifty emigrants to establish a colony upon some lands there, which they claimed to have purchased of the Indians. The governor regarded this as a breach of the treaty, for the English territory terminated and the Dutch began at the bay of Greenwich. The expedition put in at Manhattan. The energetic governor instantly arrested the leaders and held them in close confinement till they signed a promise not to proceed to the Delaware. The emigrants, thus discomfited, returned to New Haven.

At the same time Governor Stuyvesant sent a very emphatic letter to Governor Eaton of New Haven, in which he wrote:

" I shall employ force of arms and martial opposition, even to bloodshed, against all English intruders within southern New Netherland."

In this movement of the English to get a foothold upon the Delaware river, Stuyvesant thought he saw a covert purpose on their part, to dispossess the Dutch of all their possessions in America. Thinking it not improbable that it might be necessary to appeal to arms, he demanded of the authorities of Rensselaerswyck a subsidy. The patroons, who had been at great expense in colonizing the territory, deemed the demand unjust, and sent a commissioner to remonstrate against it. Stuyvesant arrested the commissioner and held him in close confinement for four months.

The Swedes were also making vigorous efforts to get possession of the beautiful lands on the Delaware. Stuyvesant, with a large suite of officers, visited that region. In very decided terms he communicated to Printz, the Swedish governor there, that the Dutch claimed the territory upon the threefold title of discovery, settlement and purchase from the natives. He then summoned all the Indian chiefs on the banks of the river, in a grand council at fort Nassau. After a "solemn conference" these chiefs ceded to the West India Company all the lands on both sides of the river to a point called by them Neuwsings, near the mouth of the bay.

The Swedes were left in possession only of a small territory surrounding their fort, called Christina. As Stuyvesant thought fort Nassau too far up the river and inconvenient of access, he demolished it. In its seclusion in the wilderness it had stood for twenty-eight years. A new fort called Casimir was erected, on the west side of the river near the present site of New Castle, four miles below the Swedish fort Christina. Having thus triumphantly accomplished his object, Stuyvesant returned to Manhattan.

CHAPTER VII.

War Between England and Holland.

GOVERNOR STUYVESANT having removed the obnoxious vice-director, had another, Johannes Dyckman, who he thought would be more subservient to his wishes, appointed in his stead. The commissary of the patroons, whom he had imprisoned at Manhattan, secreted himself on board a sloop and escaped up the river to Beaverwyck. The enraged governor seized the skipper of the sloop on his return, and inflicted upon him a heavy fine.

The patroons were now fearful that the governor would fulfill his threat of extending his authority over the extensive territory whose jurisdiction the Charter of Privileges had entrusted exclusively to the patroons. They therefore, on an appointed day, assembled the freemen and householders who bound themselves, by an oath, "to maintain and support offensively and defensively the right and jurisdiction of the colony against every one."

Among the persons who took this oath we find the name of John Baptist Van Rensselaer. He was the younger half-brother of the patroon, and probably the first of the name who came to New Netherland. It was now reported that Governor Stuyvesant himself was about to visit fort Orange, and that a new gallows was being prepared for those who should attempt to thwart his wishes. The governor soon arrived and, with his customary explicitness, informed the authorities there, that the territory by the Exemptions, allowed to the patroon, was to extend sixteen miles on one side of the river, or eight miles if both banks were occupied. He called upon them to define their boundaries, saying that he should recognize the patroons' jurisdiction only to that extent. These limits would include but a small portion of the territory which the patroons claimed by right of purchase from the Indians.

The authorities were not prepared to act upon this question without instructions from Holland. Stuyvesant would admit of no delay. He sent a party of fourteen soldiers, armed with muskets, to the patroon's house, who entered the enclosure,

7

fired a volley, and hauled down the flag of the patroon.   He then issued a decree that Beaverswyck,
which included the region now occupied by the city
of Albany, was independent of the patroon's government, and was brought under the jurisdiction of the
colony of fort Amsterdam.

Van Slechtenhorst, the patroon's bold and efficient Commissary at Rensselaerswick, ordered the
governor's placards, announcing this change, to be
torn down, and a counter proclamation, affirming
the claims of the patroon to be posted in its stead.
The governor arrested him, imprisoned him for a
time in fort Orange, and then removed him to New
Amsterdam, where he was held in close custody,
until his successor, John Baptist Van Rensselaer, was
formally appointed in his place.

At this time, 1652, there were no settlements,
and but a few scattered farmhouses between the isl-
and of Manhattan and the Catskill mountains.
Thomas Chambers had a farm at what is now Troy.
With a few neighbors he moved down the river to
"some exceedingly beautiful lands," and began the
settlement of the present county of Ulster.

Stuyvesant returning to Manhattan, forbade any
persons from buying lands of the Indians without
his permission. The large sales which had been
made to prominent individuals were declared to be

void, and the "pretended proprietors," were ordered
to return the purchase money. Should they however petition the governor, they might retain such
tracts as he and his council should permit.

By grant of the governor several new settlements
were commenced on Long Island, one at Newton,
one at Flatbush. The news had now reached
the Directors of the Company in Holland, of the
governor's very energetic measures on the Delaware,
supplanting the Swiss, demolishing fort Nassau and
erecting fort Casimir. They became alarmed lest
such violent measures might embroil them with the
Swedish government. In a letter addressed to
Stuyvesant, they wrote:

"Your journey to the South river, and what has
passed there between you and the Swedes, was very
unexpected to us, as you did not give us before so
much as a hint of your intention. We cannot give
our opinion upon it until we have heard the complaints of the Swedish governor to his queen, and
have ascertained how these have been received at
her court. We hope that our arguments, to prove
that we were the first possessors of that country,
will be acknowledged as sufficient. Time will instruct us of the design of the new-built fort Casimir
We are at a loss to conjecture for what reason it has
received this name. You ought to be on your guard

that it be well secured, so that it cannot be surprised."

The States-General were more and more dissatisfied with the measures of Governor Stuyvesant. The treaty of Hartford was severely censured. They said that the Connecticut river should have been the eastern boundary of New Netherland, and that the whole of Long Island should have been retained. Even the West India Company became convinced that it was necessary to make some concessions to the commonalty at Manhattan. They therefore communicated to Stuyvesant their consent that the "burgher government" should be established, which the committee of Nine had petitioned for in behalf of the commonalty, in 1649, and which the States-General had authorized in 1650.

By this arrangement the people were to elect seven representatives, who were to form a municipal court of justice, subject to the right of appeal to the Supreme Court of the province. The sheriff was also invested with new powers. He was to convoke and preside at the municipal court, to prosecute all offenders against the laws, and to take care that all the judgments of the court should be executed. The people at Manhattan had thus won, to a very considerable degree, the popular government which they had so long desired.

Quite to the amazement of the Directors of the West India Company, the States-General recalled Stuyvesant, ordering him to return immediately to Holland to give an account of his administration. He had been in the main the faithful agent of the Company, carrying out its wishes in opposition to popular reform. They therefore wrote to him, stating that the requirement was in violation of their charter, and requesting him "not to be in too much haste to commence his voyage, but to delay it until the receipt of further orders."

It so happened, however, that then the States-General were just on the eve of hostilities with England. It was a matter of the first importance that New Netherland should be under the rule of a governor of military experience, courage and energy. No man could excel Stuyvesant in these qualities. Yielding to the force of circumstances, the States-General revoked their recall. Thus narrowly Stuyvesant escaped the threatened humiliation.

The English government was angry with Holland for refusing to expel the royalist refugees, who, after the execution of Charles I., had taken refuge in Holland. The commerce of the Dutch Republic then covered every sea. England, to punish the Dutch and to revive her own decaying commerce, issued, by Parliamentary vote, her famous " Act of

Navigation," which was exultantly proclaimed at the old London Exchange " with sound of trumpet and beat of drum."

This Act decreed that no production of Asia, Africa or America should be brought to England, except in English vessels, manned by English crews, and that no productions of Europe should be brought to England, unless in English vessels, or in those of the country in which the imported cargoes were produced. These measures were considered very unjust by all the other nations, and especially by the Dutch, then the most commercial nation on the globe.

The States-General sent ambassadors to London to remonstrate against such hostile action ; and at the same time orders were issued for the equipment of one hundred and fifty ships of war. The States-General had not yet ratified Stuyvesant's treaty of Hartford. The ambassadors were instructed to urge that an immovable boundary line should be established between the Dutch and English possessions in America.

The reply of the English Government was not conciliatory. The English, it was said, had always been forbidden to trade in the Dutch colonies. The Dutch ought therefore to find no fault with the recent Navigation Act, from which measure the

Council did not " deem it fitting to recede." As to the colonial boundary, the ungracious reply was returned,

" The English were the first settlers in North America, from Virginia to Newfoundland. We know nothing of any Dutch plantations there, excepting a few settlers up the Hudson. We do not think it necessary at present, to settle the boundaries. It can be done hereafter, at any convenient time."

A naval war soon broke out. England, without warning, seized the ships of Holland in English ports, and impressed their crews. The Dutch war fleet was entrusted to Admiral Tromp. He was enjoined to protect the Dutch vessels from visitation or search by foreign cruisers, and not to strike his flag to English ships of war. The instructions of the commanders of the British men of war, were to compel the ships of all foreign nations whatever, to strike their colors to the British flag. England thus set up its arrogant claim to " its undoubted right to the dominion of the surrounding seas."

The English fleet, under Admiral Blake, met the Dutch fleet in the Strait of Dover, on the 29th of May, 1632, and a bloody but undecisive battle ensued. A series of terrible naval conflicts followed, with victory now on the one side and now on the

other. At length Blake, discomfited, was compelled to take refuge in the Thames. Admiral Tromp,
rather vain-gloriously, placed a broom at his mast-
head to indicate that he had swept the channel of
all English ships.

In this state of affairs the Directors wrote to
Governor Stuyvesant, saying, "Though we hope
that you have so agreed with the colonists of New
England about boundaries that we have nothing
to fear from them, still we consider it an imperious
duty to recommend you to arm and discipline all
freemen, soldiers and sailors ; to appoint officers and
places of rendezvous ; to supply them with ammunition ; and to inspect the fortifications at New Amsterdam, fort Orange and fort Casimir. To this end
we send you a fresh supply of ammunition.

"If it should happen, which we will not suppose,
that New Englanders incline to take part in these
broils, then we should advise your honor to engage
the Indians in your cause, who, we are informed,
are not partial to the English. You will also employ all such means of defence as prudence may require for your security, taking care that the merchants and inhabitants convey their property within
the forts.

"Treat them kindly, so that they may be encouraged to remain there, and to give up the thought of

returning to Holland, which would depopulate the country. It is therefore advisable to inclose the villages, at least the principal and most opulent, with breastworks and palisades to prevent surprise."

Looking into the future with prophetic eyes, which discerned the future glories of the rising republic, the Directors added, " When these colonies once become permanently established, when the ships of New Netherland ride on every part of the ocean, then numbers, now looking to that coast with eager eyes, shall be allured to embark for your island."

This prophecy is now emphatically fulfilled when often one or two thousand emigrants, from the old world, land at the Battery in a day. When the prophecy was uttered, New Amsterdam was a small straggling village of one story huts, containing about seven hundred inhabitants. The whole island of Manhattan belonged in fee to the West India Company. A municipal government was soon organized, which about the year 1653, gave birth to the city of New Amsterdam.

Holland and England were now in open and deadly warfare. It will hardly be denied by any one, that England was responsible for the conflict. The New England colonies wished to avail themselves of the opportunity to wrest New Netherland

7*

from the Dutch, and to extend their sway from
Stamford to the Chesapeake. Governor Stuyvesant
perceived his danger. He could be easily overpowered by the New England colonies. He wrote
very friendly letters to the governors, urging that,
notwithstanding the hostilities between the mother-
countries, commercial intercourse between the colonies should continue on its former peaceful footing.
At the same time he adopted very vigorous measures to be prepared for defence should he be
assailed.

Rumors reached New Amsterdam of active military preparations in progress in New England. It
was manifest that some hostile expedition was contemplated. Fort Amsterdam was repaired. The
city was enclosed by a ditch and palisade, with a
breastwork extending from the East river to the
North river. The whole body of citizens mounted
guard every night. A frigate in the harbor was
ready at any moment to spread its sails, and its
" guns were kept loaded day and night." The citizens without exception, were ordered to work upon
the defences, under penalty of fine, loss of citizen-
ship and banishment.

Thus barbaric war came again to mar all the
prosperity of the colony, and to undermine all its
foundations of growth and happiness. The Mohican

Indians, on the east side of the North river, and whose territory extended to the Connecticut, were allies of the English. Uncas, the chief of this tribe, declared that Governor Stuyvesant was plotting to arm the Narragansetts against New England. At the same time nine chiefs from the vicinity of Manhattan, sent a messenger to Stamford, who said:

"The Dutch governor has earnestly solicited the Indians in these parts, to kill all the English. But we have all refused to be hired by him, for the English have done us no harm."

The New England colonists were by no means satisfied that these charges were true. Veracity was not an Indian virtue. Cunning was a prominent trait in their character. An extraordinary meeting of commissioners was held in Boston, in April, 1653. Two messengers had been previously sent by the Massachusetts council, to interrogate three of the principal Narragansett chiefs, respecting the conduct of Governor Stuyvesant. They reported at the meeting, that the Narragansett chiefs utterly denied that Governor Stuyvesant had ever approached them with any such proposition. One of them, Ninigret, said:

"It was winter when I visited the Dutch governor. I stood the great part of a winter's day, knocking at his door. He would neither open it nor suffer others to open it, to let me in. I found no proposal to stir me up against the English, my friends."

Mixam, another of these chiefs, replied, "I do not know of any plot that is intended by the Dutch governor against the English, my friends."

The third of the chiefs, who was conferred with, Pessacus, was still more emphatic in his denial. "Though I am far away," he said, "from the governor of the Dutch, I am not willing for the sake of pleasing the English, to invent any falsehood against him."

The result of these investigations led some to suppose that individuals among the English had originated these rumors, and had bribed some of the Indian chiefs to false charges that they might instigate the governors to send out an expedition for the capture of New Netherland.

Still the Council was unsatisfied, and retained its suspicions. Governor Stuyvesant, hearing of the charges against him, wrote at once to the governors of Massachusetts and New Haven, unequivocally denying the plot, and offering to come himself to Boston " to consider and examine what may be charged, and his answers." Should the Council prefer, he would send a delegate to Boston, or they might send delegates to Manhattan to investigate the whole affair.

The Council decided to send three commissioners, men of note, to Manhattan. At the same time an army of five hundred men was ordered to be organized "for the first expedition," should "God call the colonies to make war against the Dutch."

The New England agents were hospitably received at New Amsterdam. They urged that the meeting should be held in one of the New England colonies, where Stuyvesant "should produce evidence to clear himself from the charges against him." He was to be regarded as guilty until he proved himself innocent.

The Puritan agents appear to great disadvantage in the conference which ensued. "They seem to have visited the Dutch," writes Mr. Brodhead, "as inquisitors, to collect evidence criminating the Dutch and to collect no other evidence. And, with peculiar assurance, they saw no impropriety in requiring the authorities of New Netherland, in their own capital, to suspend their established rules of law in favor of those of New England."

Governor Stuyvesant repressed every expression of impatience, and urged the most friendly overtures. It may be said that it was manifestly for his interest to do so, for the Dutch colonies were quite powerless compared with the united colonies of New England. The New England agents ungraciously repelled his advances, and at length abruptly terminated the conference without giving the governor an opportunity to prove his innocence. At nine o'clock in the evening they suddenly took leave of New Amsterdam, declining the most friendly invitations to remain, and "cloaking their sudden departure under pretence of the day of election to be held this week at Boston." They left behind them the following menace :

"The Commissioners conclude their negotiation by declaring that if you shall offer any injury to any of the English in these parts, whether by yourselves or by the Indians, either upon the national quarrel, or by reason of any differences depending between the United English Colonies and yourselves, that, as the Commissioners will do no wrong, so they may not suffer their countrymen to be oppressed upon any such account."

The morning after this unfriendly retirement of the agents, Governor Stuyvesant dispatched a messenger to Boston, with a letter containing a very full reply to the grievances of which the New England colonists complained. In this letter, which bears the impress of frankness and honesty, he says,

"What your worships lay unto our charge are

false reports and feigned informations. Your honored messengers might, if they had pleased, have informed themselves of the truth of this, and might also have obtained more friendly satisfaction and security, concerning our real intentions, if they had pleased to stay a day or two with us, to have heard and considered further of these articles."

On their way home, the New England agents stopped at Flushing, Stamford and New Haven, to collect all the evidence they could against Governor Stuyvesant. The hearsay stories of the Indians they carefully picked up. Still the only point ascertained, of any moment was, that Governor Stuyvesant had told an Englishman, one Robert Coe, that if the English attacked him, he should try to get the Indians to come to his aid ; and that he had said the same to William Alford.

This was all the evidence the agents could find against the governor. He had made these declarations without any purpose of concealment. He had been instructed to pursue this course by the Amsterdam Directors. The New England colonists had in their Pequod war, set the example of employing Indian allies. This repulsive feature in the British colonial administration continued until the close of the war of the Revolution. .

Captain John Underhill, an Englishman, who had

obtained considerable renown in the Pequod war,
becoming dissatisfied with some ecclesiastical cen-
sure which he had incurred, petitioned Governor
Stuyvesant for permission to reside, with a few other
families in New Netherland, under the protection
of the Dutch, offering to take the oath of allegiance
which was required of all foreigners. His request
was promptly granted. It was the liberal policy of
the Dutch government not to exclude foreigners
from any privileges which the Hollanders themselves
enjoyed. Underhill was now residing at Hempstead,
Long Island. His restless spirit, ever eager for
change, seized upon the present moment as a fitting
opportunity to wrest from the Dutch their portion
of Long Island, and pass it over to his countrymen.
In violation of his oath he issued a treasonable proclamation, in which he said,

"You are called upon to abjure the iniquitous
government of Peter Stuyvesant over the inhabitants residing on Long Island. His rule is too
grievous for any brave Englishman and good christian to tolerate any longer. All honest hearts that
seek the glory of God and his peace and prosperity,
are exhorted to throw off this tyrannical yoke. Accept and submit ye then to the Parliament of England; and beware of becoming traitors to one

another for the sake of your own quiet and welfare."

This proclamation did not meet with a cordial response. Underhill fled to Rhode Island. Here he received from Boston a commission, "to take all Dutch ships and vessels as shall come into his power, and to defend himself from the Dutch and all enemies of the commonwealth of England."

The report of the agents who had visited Manhattan was such that the General Court at Boston voted that they were not "called upon to make a present war with the Dutch."

There were eight commissioners from the New England colonies in Boston. Notwithstanding this decision of the General Court, six of them were in favor of instant war. They sent back to Governor Stuyvesant an abusive and defiant reply, in which they said,

"Your confident denials of the barbarous plot with which you are charged will weigh little in the balance against the evidence, so that we must still require and seek due satisfaction and security."

The Connecticut colonists were ever looking with a wistful eye to the rich lands west of them. The Court at New Haven and that at Hartford sent messengers to Massachusetts to urge that "by war if no other means will serve, the Dutch, at and

about the Manhattoes, who have been and still are
like to prove injurious, may be removed." The
General Court nobly replied, " We cannot act in so
weighty a concernment, as to send forth men to
shed blood, unless satisfied that God calls for it.
And then it must be clear and not doubtful."

" In speaking of these events Mr. Brodhead says,
" At the annual meeting of the Commissioners, Massachusetts maintained her proud position with a
firmness which almost perilled the stability of the
confederation. A bitter altercation, between the
representatives of the other colonies and the General Court, was terminated by an ambiguous concession which nevertheless averted hostilities.

" The Connecticut governments seemed animated
by the most vindictive feelings; and their own recent
historian laments the refusal of the Massachusetts
authorities to bear part in an offensive war against
New Netherland, as an 'indelible stain upon their
honor as men, and upon their morals as christians.'"

There was a strong party in favor of war as the
only means of wresting the magnificent domain of
New Netherland from the Dutch and annexing it to
the New England possessions. The majestic Hudson was greatly coveted, as it opened to commerce
vast and unknown regions of the interior.

Hartford and New Haven discussed the question

if they were not strong enough without the aid of Massachusetts to subdue the Dutch. Stamford and Fairfield commenced raising volunteers on their own account, and appointed one Ludlow as their leader. A petition was sent to the home government, the Commonwealth over which Oliver Cromwell was then presiding, praying "that the Dutch be either removed or, so far, at least, subjected that the colonies may be free from injurious affronts and secured against the dangers and mischievous effects which daily grow upon them by their plotting with the Indians and furnishing them with arms against the English."

In conclusion they entreated that two or three frigates be sent out, and that Massachusetts be commanded to assist the other colonies to clear the coast "of a nation with which the English cannot either mingle or set under their government, nor so much as live near without danger of their lives and all their comforts in this world."

To fan this rising flame of animosity against the Dutch, a rancorous pamphlet was published in London, entitled, "The second part of the Amboyna Tragedy; or a faithful account of a bloody, treacherous and cruel plot of the Dutch in America, purporting the total ruin and murder of all the English colonists in New England; extracted from the various letters lately written from New England to different merchants in London."

This was indeed an inflammatory pamphlet. The most violent language was used. The Dutch were accused of the "devilish project" of trying to rouse the savages to a simultaneous assault upon all the New England colonists. The crime was to be perpetrated on Sunday morning, when they should be collected in their houses of worship. Men, women and children were to be massacred, and the buildings laid in ashes.

The Amsterdam Directors had this "most infamous and lying libel," translated into their own language and sent a copy to Governor Stuyvesant and his council, saying:

"We wish that your honors may see what stratagems that nation employs, not only to irritate the populace, but the whole world if possible and to stir it up against us."

The position of Governor Stuyvesant had become exceedingly uncomfortable. He was liable at any day to have from abroad war's most terrible storm burst upon him. And the enemy might come in such force that he would be utterly unable to make any effectual resistance. On the other hand the Dutch settlements were composed of emigrants from all lands. Many Englishmen, dissatisfied with the rigid rule of the New England colonies, had taken their residence in New Netherland.

The arbitrary rule of Stuyvesant was obnoxious to the majority of his subjects, and they were increasingly clamorous for a more liberal and popular government. On the 16th of December, 1630, a very important popular convention was held at New Amsterdam, composed of delegates from eight towns. There were nineteen delegates, ten of whom were Dutch and nine English. Unanimously they avowed fealty to the government of Holland. But they remonstrated against the establishment of an arbitrary government; and complained that laws had been enacted without the consent of the people.

"This," said they, " is contrary to the granted privilege of the Netherland government and odious to every free-born man; and especially so to those whom God has placed in a free state in newly-settled lands, who are entitled to claim laws not transcending, but resembling as near as possible those of the Netherlands."

There were several minor offences enumerated to which we need not here refer. The memorial was drawn up by an Englishman, George Baxter. The imperious Stuyvesant was greatly annoyed by this document. To weaken its effect, he declared that the delegates had no authority to act or even to meet upon such questions.   He endeavored to rouse national prejudice against the document by saying:

"The most ancient colony of Manhattan, the colonies of Rensselaerswyck and Staten Island and the settlements at Beaverswyck and on the South river are too prudent to subscribe to all that has been projected by an Englishman; as if among the Netherlands' nation there is no one sagacious and expert enough to draw up a remonstrance to the Director and council."

CHAPTER VIII.

Another Indian War.

Conflict Between the Governor and the Citizens.—Energy of the Governor.—His Measures of Defence.—Action of the English Colonies.—Claims of the Government of Sweden.—Fort Casimir captured by the Swedes.—Retaliation.—Measures for the recapture of Fort Casimir.—Shooting a Squaw.—Its Consequences.—The Ransom of Prisoners.—Complaints of the Swedish Governor.—Expedition from Sweden.—Its Fate.

THERE was a brief but bitter controversy between the governor and the convention, when the governor ordered the body to disperse, " on pain of our highest displeasure." " We derive our authority," said he, " from God, and from the Company, not from a few ignorant subjects. And we alone can call the inhabitants together." These decisive measures did not stifle the popular voice. Petitions were sent to the Company in Holland, full of complaints against the administration of Stuyvesant, and imploring its intervention to secure the redress of the grievances which were enumerated.

An able man, Francois le Bleuw, was sent to Holland with these documents, with instructions to do everything in his power to procure the reforms they urged. Though the citizens of New Amsterdam had, for a year, enjoyed a limited municipal government, they were by no means satisfied with what they had thus far attained. What they claimed, and reasonably claimed, were the larger franchises enjoyed by the cities in the fatherland.

The condition of New Netherland, at the commencement of the year 1654, was very precarious. The troubled times, as is ever the case, had called out swarms of pirates and robbers, who infested the shores of Long Island, inflicting the most cruel excesses upon the unprotected inhabitants. The English residents in the Dutch colonies were numerous, and they were ripe for revolt. The Dutch themselves were uttering loud murmurs. The governor acted with his accustomed energy. Several vessels were fitted out to act against the pirates. Many of these pirates professed to be privateersmen, serving the Commonwealth of England. It was suspected that the English residents were communicating with the freebooters, who were chiefly their own countrymen.

A proclamation was issued prohibiting all persons, under penalty of banishment and the confiscation of goods, from harboring the outlaws. Every third man was detailed to act as a minute man whenever required ; and the whole population was pledged for the public defence. At the same time, to prevent any misunderstanding, messengers were sent to Connecticut to inform the colonial authorities there, that these measures were adopted solely for the protection of their commerce and the punishment of robbery.

In February of this year, a church was organized at Flatbush. Domine Polhemus was chosen pastor, with a salary of six hundred guilders. A cruciform wooden church was erected, sixty feet long and twenty-eight feet wide. This was the first Reformer Dutch Church on Long Island. The Lutherans had now become quite numerous in New Amsterdam. They petitioned for liberty to organize a church. Stuyvesant, a zealous Calvinist, declined, saying that he was bound by his oath to tolerate no other religion openly than the Reformed. In this intolerance he was sustained by the Company in Holland.

Oliver Cromwell now decided to carry the war against Holland into the New World. He sent word to the governors of the New England Colonists that he was about to dispatch war ships to the coasts of America, and he called upon them to give their utmost assistance for gaining the Manhattoes and other places under the power of the Dutch."

Four armed ships were soon crossing the Atlantic. The expedition was entrusted to Major Sedgwick and John Leverett. They were directed to enter some good port in New England, where they were to ascertain whether the colonial governments would join in vindicating the English right and in extirpating the Dutch.

"Being come to the Manhattoes," wrote secretary Thurlow, "you shall, by surprise, open force, or otherwise, endeavor to take the place. You have power to give fair quarter in case it be rendered upon summons without opposition. If the Lord give his blessing, you shall not use cruelty to the inhabitants, but encourage those who are willing to remain under the English government, and give liberty to others to transport themselves to Europe."

Governor Stuyvesant received early intelligence of the projected expedition, and immediately convened his council. The danger was imminent. The Dutch alone could oppose but feeble resistance. The English in the Dutch colony, though they had sworn allegiance, would probably join their countrymen. "To invite them," Governor Stuyvesant said, "to aid us, would be bringing the Trojan horse within our walls." After much anxious deliberation, it was decided to enlist a force of seventy men, "silently and without beat of drum," and to lay in supplies to stand a siege.

The danger roused the spirit of patriotism. The Dutch rallied with great unanimity and, spade in hand, worked heartily on the fortifications. They were all conscious, however, that treason lurked within their walls.

Several of the New England colonies responded quite eagerly to the appeal of Cromwell. New Haven pledged herself to the most zealous efforts. Connecticut promised two hundred men, and even five hundred rather than that the enterprise should fail. Plymouth ordered fifty men into the service, entrusting the command to Captain Miles Standish and Captain Thomas Willett. It is worthy of notice that the Plymouth people made an apology for this action, saying:

"We concur in hostile measures against our ancient Dutch neighbors only in reference unto the national quarrel."

Massachusetts gave a reluctant consent that five hundred volunteers against the Dutch should be raised within their jurisdiction.

Just as the fleet was about to sail from Boston, on this expedition, the result of which could not be doubtful, a ship entered the port with the announcement that peace had been concluded between England and Holland. This of course put a stop to any farther hostile action. The welcome news was soon conveyed to Governor Stuyvesant. He was quite overjoyed in its reception. The glad tidings were published from the City Hall, with ringing of bell and all other public demonstrations of satisfaction.

The 12th of August was appointed as a day of general thanksgiving to God for his great goodness. In his proclamation, the Governor devoutly exclaimed:

"Praise the Lord, O England's Jerusalem and Netherland's zion, praise ye the Lord! He hath secured your gates and blessed your possessions with peace, even here where the threatened torch of war was lighted, where the waves reached our lips and subsided only through the power of the Almighty."

From this moral conflict, which came so near being a physical one, Stuyvesant emerged very victorious. The Company had ever been disposed to sympathize with him in his measures. The delegate Le Bleuw, who had carried charges against him to Holland, was almost rudely repulsed, and was forbidden to return to New Netherland. The Directors of the Company wrote to the Governor:

"We are unable to discover in the whole remonstrance one single point to justify complaint. You ought to have acted with more vigor against the ringleaders of the gang, and not to have condescended to answer protests with protests. It is therefore our express command that you punish what has occurred as it deserves, so that others may be deterred in future, from following such examples."

To the citizens they wrote, "We enjoin it upon you that you conduct yourselves quietly and peaceably, submit yourselves to the government placed over you, and in no wise allow yourselves to hold particular convention with the English or others, in matters of form or deliberation on affairs of state, which do not appertain to you, or attempt any alteration in the state and its government."

A ferry was established to convey passengers from one side of the river to the other. The licensed ferryman was bound to keep suitable boats and also a lodge on each side of the river to protect passengers from the weather. The toll established by law, was for a wagon and two horses one dollar; for a wagon and one horse eighty cents; a savage, male or female, thirty cents; each other person fifteen cents.

When Stuyvesant was preparing to defend New Netherland from the English, he encountered another great annoyance. It will be remembered

that the Swedish government claimed the territory
on the South, or Delaware river, upon which the
Dutch governor had erected Fort Casimir. Gerrit
Bikker was in command of the fort, with a garrison
of twelve men. On the morning of the first of June,
1654, a strange sail was seen in the offing. A small
party was sent out in a boat, to reconnoitre. They
returned with the tidings that it was a Swedish ship
full of people, with a new governor; and that they
had come to take possession of the place, affirming
that the fort was on land belonging to the Swedish
government.

Bikker with his small garrison, and almost destitute of ammunition, could make no resistance.
Twenty or thirty soldiers landed from the Swedish
ship, entered the open gate of the fort and took
possession of the place. John Rising the commander of the ship, stated that he was obeying the
orders of his government; that the territory belonged to Sweden, and that neither the States-General of the Netherlands nor the West India Company had authorized Governor Stuyvesant to erect
a fort upon that spot.

The garrison was disarmed, two shotted guns
were fired over the works in token of their capture,
and the name of the fort was changed to Trinity, as
it was on Trinity Sunday that the fort was taken

A skilful engineer immediately employed many hands in strengthening the ramparts. The region was called New Sweden, and John Rising assumed his office as governor. Courteously he sent word to Governor Stuyvesant of his arrival and of his capture of the forts. He also summoned the chiefs of the neighboring tribes and entered into a treaty of friendship with them. Within a month he announced to the home government that the population of New Sweden had risen to three hundred and sixty-eight. "I hope," he added, "we may be able to preserve them in order and in duty, and to constrain them if necessary. I will do in this respect, all that depends upon me. We will also endeavor to shut up the river."

Governor Stuyvesant was very indignant, in view of what he deemed the pusillanimous conduct of Bikker in "this dishonorable surrender of the fort." It was in vain for him to attempt its recovery. But with an eagle eye and an agitated mind he watched for an opportunity to retaliate.

About the middle of September, a Swedish ship, the Golden Shark, bound for the Delaware river, under command of Captain Elswyck, entered Sandy Hook and anchored behind Staten Island. The captain had made a mistake and supposed that he had entered the mouth of South river. Discovering

his error, he sent a boat up to Manhattan for a pi-
lot.

Stuyvesant's long-looked-for hour had come.
He arrested the boat's crew, and sent them all to
the guard-house. He also seized the Shark and
transferred her cargo to the Company's magazine on
shore. He then sent a courteous message to Governor Rising, at New Sweden, inviting him to visit
New Amsterdam, "to arrange and settle some unexpected differences." He promised him a hospita-
ble reception, but declared that he should detain the
Swedish ship and cargo, "until a reciprocal restitution shall have been made." Governor Rising declined the invitation, not deeming it judicious to place
himself so effectually in the power of his impetuous
antagonist.

Upon the capture of fort Casimir, Governor Stuyvesant had immediately sent word of the occurrence
to the Amsterdam Directors. In November he
received their reply. It was, in brief, as follows:

"We hardly know whether we are more astonished at the audacious enterprise of the Swedes in
taking our fort on the South river, or at the cowardly
surrender of it by our commander, which is nearly
insufferable. He has acted very unfaithfully, yea
treacherously. We entreat you to exert every nerve
to avenge that injury, not only by restoring affairs

to their former situation, but by driving the Swedes from every side of the river. We have put in commission two armed ships, the King Solomon and the Great Christopher. The drum is beaten daily in the streets of Amsterdam for volunteers. And orders are given for the instant arrest of Bikker.

Stuyvesant adopted vigorous measures to co-operate with the little fleet upon its arrival, in its warfare against New Sweden. The 25th of August, 1655, was set apart as a day of fasting and prayer, "to implore the only bountiful God, that it may please him to bless the projected enterprise, under-taken only for the greater security, extension and consolidation of this province, and to render it pros-perous and successful to the glory of his name."

Enlistments were pushed with great energy. Three North river vessels were chartered, pilots were engaged and provisions and ammunition laid in store. A French privateer, L'Esperance, which chanced to enter the harbor of New Amsterdam at this time, was also engaged for the service.

It seems hardly consistent with the religious character of Stuyvesant and with his prayers for the divine blessing, that the Lord's day should have been chosen for the sailing of the expedition. But on the first Sunday in September, after the morning sermon, the sails of the little squadron of seven

8*

vessels were unfurled and the fleet put to sea, containing a military force of about seven hundred men. Governor Stuyvesant in person, commanded the expedition. He was accompanied by the Vice-Governor, De Lille, and by Domine Megapolensis, as chaplain.

On Friday morning they entered the Delaware river, and with favoring wind and tide, sailed up beyond fort Casimir, and landed their forces about a mile above. A flag of truce was promptly sent to the fort, demanding "the direct restitution of our own property." Some parleying occupied the time during the day, while Stuyvesant was landing his batteries. The next morning the Swedish commander, convinced of the folly of any further attempt at resistance, went on board the Balance and signed a capitulation. The victor was generous in his terms. The Swedes were allowed to remove their artillery; twelve men were to march out with full arms and accoutrements; all the rest retained their side-arms, and the officers held their personal property.

At noon the Dutch, with pealing bugles and flying banners again entered upon possession of the fort. Many of the Swedes took the oath of allegiance to the New Netherland government. The next day was Sunday. Chaplain Megapolensis

preached a sermon to the troops. But a short distance above fort Casimir there was another Swedish
fort called Christina. It was not denied that the
Swedes had a legitimate title to that land. Indeed
after the Company in Holland had sent directions to
Stuyvesant to drive the Swedes from the river, they
sent to him another order modifying these instructions. In this dispatch they said:

"You may allow the Swedes to hold the land
on which fort Christina is built, with a garden to
cultivate the tobacco, because it appears that they
made this purchase with the previous consent of
the Company, provided said Swedes will conduct
themselves as good subjects of our government."

But the Swedish Governor, Rising, having lost
fort Casimir, re-assembled his forces and strengthened his position in Fort Christina, which was two
miles farther up the river. This fort was about
thirty-five miles below the present site of Philadelphia, on a small stream called Christina creek. The
fleet anchored at the mouth of the Brandywine, and
invested the fort on all sides. The Swedes outside
of the fort were ruthlessly pillaged; a battery was
erected and the fort summoned to surrender. Resistance was hopeless. The articles of capitulation
were soon signed between the victor and the van-
quished.

"The Swedes marched out with their arms, colors flying, matches lighted, drums beating and fifes playing; and the Dutch took possession of the fort, hauled down the Swedish flag and hoisted their own."

The Swedes, who to the number of about two hundred had settled in that vincinity, were allowed to remain in the country, if they wished to do so, upon condition of taking the oath of allegiance to the Dutch authorities. Thus the Swedish dominion on the South river was brought to an end. This was the most powerful military expedition which had ever moved from any of the colonies. The Swedes had held their independent position on the Delaware but about seventeen years. Leaving an agent, as temporary commandant, Stuyvesant returned triumphantly to fort Amsterdam.

And now for ten years there had been peace with the Indians, when a gross outrage again roused their savage natures to revenge. The Indians, ever accustomed to roam the forest, and to gather fruits, nuts and game wherever they could find them, had not very discriminating views of the rights of private property. Ensign Van Dyck, the former treasurer, and one of the most noted men in the colony, detected an Indian woman in his orchard gathering peaches. Inhumanly he shot her dead. This roused all the neighboring tribes, and they united to avenge her death. There was certainly something chivalrous in this prompt combination of the warriors not to allow, what they deemed the murder of a sister, to pass unpunished.

Taking advantage of the absence of Governor Stuyvesant, with nearly all the military force he could raise, on his expedition to the South river, sixty-four war canoes, containing nineteen hundred armed Indians, were at midnight on the fifteenth of September, stealthily paddled into the waters surrounding fort Amsterdam. They were picked warriors from eight tribes. The night was dark, and the sighing of the wind through the tree tops and the breaking of the surf upon the beach added to the deep repose of the sleepers.

The Indians landed and stealthily crept through the silent streets; and yet, from some unexplained cause, they made no attack. Gradually the inhabitants were awakened, and there was a rapid assembling of the principal men within the fort. Several of the chiefs were called before them. They gave no satisfactory account of the object of their formidable visit, and uttered no threats. On the contrary they promised to withdraw before night, to Nutten Island, as Governor's island was then called. Still, watching their opportunity, one of the warriors pierced the bosom of Van Dyck with an arrow.

The cry of murder rang through the streets. The inhabitants were prepared for the not unexpected emergency. The military rushed from the fort, and a fierce battle ensued. The Indians, leaving three of their warriors dead in the streets, and having killed five white men and wounded three others, were driven to their canoes, and crossed over the North river to the Jersey shore.

And now their savage natures burst forth unrestrained. The flourishing little villages of Pavonia and Hoboken were instantly in flames. A general scene of massacre and destruction ensued. Men, women and children fell alike before the bullet, the arrow and the tomahawk. The inhabitants of fort Amsterdam in anguish witnessed the massacre, but could render no assistance. Nearly all their armed men were far away on the Delaware.

The savages, elated with success, crossed over to Staten island. The scattered settlements there numbered about ninety souls. There were eleven farms in a high state of cultivation, and several plantations. The settlers had received warning of their danger, perhaps by the flames and musketry of Hoboken and Pavonia, perhaps by some messenger from fort Amsterdam. Sixty-seven of them succeeded in reaching some stronghold where they were able to defend themselves. The rest, twenty-three in number, were cut off by the savages. The buildings of twenty-eight farms and plantations were laid in ashes and the crops destroyed.

For three days these merciless Indians had free range, with scarcely any opposition. During this time one hundred of the Dutch were killed, one hundred and fifty were taken prisoners, and more than three hundred were deprived of house, clothes and food. Six hundred cattle and a vast amount of grain were destroyed. The pecuniary value of the damage inflicted amounted to over eighty thousand dollars.

Such were the consequences which resulted from the folly and crime of one man in shooting an Indian woman who was purloining peaches from his orchard. Terror spread far and wide. The farmers with their families, fled from all directions to fort Amsterdam for protection. The feeble settlements on Long island were abandoned in dismay. Prowling bands of savages wandered over the island of Manhattan, burning and destroying. No one dared to venture to any distance from the fort. An express was dispatched to South river to inform Governor Stuyvesant of the peril of the colony, and to implore his return. This led to the hurried close of the transactions on the Delaware, and probably secured for the Swedes more favorable terms of capitulation than they would otherwise have obtained.

The return of Governor Stuyvesant with his military force, reassured the colonists. In such an hour his imperious nature hesitated not a moment in assuming the dictatorship. The one man power, so essential on the field of battle, seemed requisite in these scenes of peril. There was no time for deliberation. Prompt and energetic action was necessary.

The governor sent soldiers to the outer settlements; forbade any vessel to leave the harbor, forced into the ranks every man capable of bearing arms, and imposed a heavy tax to meet the expense of strengthening the fortifications. Several persons, who were about to sail for Europe, protested against being thus detained. Governor Stuyvesant fined them each ten dollars for disrespect to the established authorities, and contemptuously advised them to "possess their souls in patience."

The savages found their captives an incumbrance. Winter was approaching and provisions were scarce. They sent one of their prisoners, an influential man, captain Pos, who had been superintendent of the colony on Staten island, to propose the ransom of those captured for a stipulated amount of powder and balls. As captain Pos did not return as soon as was expected, another messenger was sent, and soon one of the chiefs returned to Governor Stuyvesant, fourteen Dutch men, women and children, as a present in token of his good will, and asking that a *present* of powder and ball might be forwarded to him.

The governor sent in return some ammunition and two Indian captives and promised to furnish more ammunition when other christians should be brought in.

Three envoys from New Amsterdam visited the savages bearing these presents. They were received with the courtesies which civilized nations accord to a flag of truce. In this way twenty-eight more captives were ransomed. The promise was given that others should be soon brought in. Governor Stuyvesant inquired at what price they would release all the remaining prisoners en masse, or what they would ask for each individual. They deliberated upon the matter and then replied that they would deliver up twenty-eight prisoners for seventy-eight pounds of powder, and forty staves of lead.

The governor immediately sent the amount, and hoping to excite their generosity, added as a present in token of friendly feeling, thirty-five pounds of powder and ten staves of lead. But the savages did not appreciate this kindness. They returned the twenty-eight prisoners and no more.

The governor of the Swedish colony on the Delaware arrived at New Amsterdam with a numerous suite, awaiting their transportation to Europe according to the terms of the capitulation. He was in very ill humor, and Governor Stuyvesant found it impossible to please him. He entered bitter complaints against the governor, declaring that the articles of the late treaty had been grossly violated.

"In Christina," said he, "the women were violently driven out of their houses. The oxen, cows and other animals were butchered. Even the horses were wantonly shot. The whole country was desolated. Your men carried off even my own property, and we were left without means of defence against the savages. No proper accommodations have been provided for me and my suite at New Amsterdam, and our expenses have not been defrayed."

With much dignity Governor Stuyvesant vindicated himself. "I offered," he said, "to leave fort Christina in your possession, but you refused it. I am not responsible for any property for which I have not given a receipt. On account of your high station, I offered more than once to entertain you in my own house. As this did not satisfy you, you were induced to reside in one of the principal houses of the city. There you indulged in unmannerly threats that you would return and destroy this place. This so annoyed the people of the house that, for peace sake, they abandoned their lodgings.

" The rumors of these threats reached the ears of the captains of the small vessels, and the passengers with whom you were to embark. They did not deem it safe to take you and your suite, with such a large number of dependents. They feared to land you in England or France, unless they should chance to meet some English or French vessel in the Channel. We entered into no obligation to defray your expenses or those of your unusual suite."

Soon after this Governor Rising and his attendants were embarked for Europe in two vessels. A narrative was, at the same time, sent to the fatherland of the recent Indian troubles. The defenceless condition of the country was explained and assistance earnestly implored.

There were still a number of captives held by the Indian tribes who dwelt among the Highlands. The question was anxiously deliberated, in the Council, respecting the best mode of recovering them. One only, Van Tienhoven, was in favor of war. But Governor Stuyvesant said,

" The recent war is to be attributed to the rashness of a few hot-headed individuals. It becomes us to reform ourselves, to abstain from all that is wrong, and to protect our villages with proper defences. Let us build block-houses wherever they are needed and not permit any armed Indian to enter the European settlements."

The Long Island Indians sent a delegation to New Amsterdam declaring that for ten years, since 1645, they had been the friends of the Dutch, and had done them no harm, "not even to the value of a dog." They sent, as a present, a bundle of wampum in token of the friendship of the chiefs of the Eastern tribes. But the up-river Indians continued sullen. With their customary cunning or sagacity they retained quite a number of captives, holding them as pledges to secure themselves from the vengeance of the Dutch. There was no hope of liberating them by war, since the Indians would never deliver up a white captive in exchange for prisoners of their own tribes. And upon the first outbreak of war the unfortunate Dutch prisoners would be conveyed to inaccessible depths of the forests.

The Dutch settlers had scattered widely, on farms and plantations. Thus they were peculiarly exposed to attacks from the Indians, and could render each other but little assistance. As a remedy for this evil, Governor Stuyvesant issued a proclamation ordering all who lived in secluded places in the country to assemble and unite themselves in villages before the ensuing spring, "after the fashion," as he said, "of our New England neighbors."

In Sweden, before the tidings of the fall of fort Casimir had reached that country, an expedition had been fitted out for the South river, conveying one hundred and thirty emigrants. Stuyvesant, on learning of their arrival, forbade them to land. He dispatched a vessel and a land force, to capture the Swedish ship the Mercury, and bring it with all the passengers to fort Amsterdam. Having disposed of her cargo, the vessel and all the Swedish soldiers it bore, were sent back to Europe.

In obedience to orders from home, Stuyvesant erected a fort at Oyster Bay, on the north side of Long island. In the instructions he received he was enjoined, " to maintain, by force, if necessary, the integrity of the Dutch province, the boundaries of which have just been formally confirmed by the States-General."

The Directors added, "We do not hesitate to approve of your expedition on the South river, and its happy termination. We should not have been displeased, however, if such a formal capitulation for the surrender of the forts had not taken place, but that the whole business had been transacted in a manner similar to that of which the Swedes set us an example when they made themselves masters of fort Casimir."

CHAPTER IX.

An Energetic Administration.

WAR would doubtless have arisen, between Sweden and Holland, in view of transactions on South river, had not all the energies of Sweden been then called into requisition in a war with Poland. The Swedish government contented itself with presenting a vigorous memorial to the States-General, which for eight years was renewed without accomplishing any redress.

The vice-governor resided at fort Orange, in a two story house, the upper floor of which was used as a court-room. This station was the principal mart for the fur trade, which had now become so considerable that upwards of thirty-five thousand beaver skins were exported during the year 1656.

A survey of the city of New Amsterdam was

made this year, which showed that there were one
hundred and twenty houses, and a population of one
thousand souls. A man like Stuyvesant, the warm
advocate of arbitrary power, would almost of necessity, be religiously intolerant. Zealously devoted to
the Reformed church, and resolved to have unity
in religion, notwithstanding the noble toleration
which existed in Holland, he issued a proclamation
forbidding any one from holding a religious meeting not in harmony with the Reformed church.

Any preacher, who should violate this ordinance
was to be subjected to a penalty of one hundred
pounds. Any one who should attend such a meeting was to be punished by a penalty of twenty-five
pounds.

This law was rigorously enforced. Recusants
were fined and imprisoned. Complaints were sent
to Holland, and the governor was severely rebuked
for his bigotry.

"We would fain," the Directors wrote to Stuyvesant, "not have seen your worship's hand set to
the placard against the Lutherans, nor have heard
that you oppressed them with the imprisonments
of which they have complained to us. It has always
been our intention to let them enjoy all calmness
and tranquillity. Wherefore you will not hereafter
publish any similar placards, without our previous

consent, but allow all the free exercise of their religion within their own houses." ·

But Stuyvesant was a man born to govern, not be governed. He was silent respecting the instructions he had received from home. When the Lutherans informed him that the Directors of the Company had ordered that the same toleration should exist in New Netherland which was practiced in the fatherland, he firmly replied that he must wait for further explanations, and that in the mean time his ordinance against public conventicles must be executed.

At Flushing a cobbler from Rhode Island, a baptist, William Wickendam by name, ventured to preach, "and even went with the people into the river and dipped them." He was fined one thousand pounds and ordered to be banished. As he was a poor man the debt was remitted, but he was obliged to leave the province.

It will be remembered that thus far nearly all the operations of the Dutch, in the New World, had been performed under the authority of Dutch merchants, called "The West India Company." Their chartered powers were very great. Only in a subordinate degree were they subject to the control of the States-General.

At this time there was a very cruel persecution commenced by the Duke of Savoy against the Wal-

denses.   Hundreds of them fled to the city of
Amsterdam, in Holland, which was then the refuge
for the persecuted of all nations.   They were received
with the most noble hospitality.   The city government not only gave them an asylum, but voted large
sums from its treasury, for their support.

Carrying out this policy, the city decided to establish a colony of its own in New Netherland, to
be composed mainly of these Waldenses.   The
municipal authorities purchased of the West India
Company, for seven hundred guilders, all the land
on the west side of South river, from Christina kill
to Bombay Hook.   This gave a river front of about
forty miles, running back indefinitely into the
interior.   This region was named New Amstel.
The colonists were offered a free passage, ample
farms on the river, and provisions and clothing for
one year.   The city also agreed to send out "a
proper person for a schoolmaster, who shall also read
the holy Scriptures in public and set the Psalms."
A church was to be organized so soon as there were
two hundred inhabitants in the colony.

The Company wrote to Stuyvesant saying, "The
confidence we feel about the success and increase of
this new colony of which we hope to see some
prominent features next spring, when to all appearance, large numbers of the exiled Waldenses will

flock thither, as to an asylum, induces us to send you orders to endeavor to purchase of the Indians, before it can be accomplished by any other nation, all that tract of land situated between the South river and the Hook of the North river, to provide establishments for these emigrants."

On Christmas day of 1656, three vessels containing one hundred and sixty emigrants, sailed from the Texel. A wintry storm soon separated them. The principal ship, the Prince Maurice, which had the largest number of passengers, after a long voyage, was wrecked on the South coast of Long island, near Fire island inlet, in the neighborhood of the present town of Islip. It was midnight when the ship struck. As soon as it was light the passengers and crew succeeded in reaching the shore in their boats through the breakers and through vast masses of floating ice.

They found upon the shore a bleak, barren, tree-less waste, "without weeds, grass or timber of any sort to make a fire." It was bitter cold. A fierce wind swept the ocean and the land, and the sea ran so high that it was expected every moment the ship would go to pieces. These poor emigrants thus suddenly huddled upon the icy land, without food and without shelter, were in imminent peril of perishing from cold and starvation.

Their sufferings were so terrible that they were rejoiced to see some Indians approaching over the wide plains, though they knew not whether the savages would prove hostile or friendly. But the Indians came like brothers, aided them in every way, and dispatched two swift runners across the island to inform Governor Stuyvesant of the calamity. Some sails were brought on shore, with which a temporary shelter from the piercing blast was constructed, and enough food was secured to save from absolute starvation.

The energetic governor immediately dispatched nine or ten lighters to their assistance, and with needful supplies proceeded in person to the scene of the disaster. Thus nearly all the cargo was saved and the passengers were transported to New Amsterdam. There were one hundred and twenty-five passengers on board the Prince Maurice, seventy-six of whom were women and children. Another ship, the Gilded Beaver, was chartered at New Amsterdam which conveyed them all safely, after a five days' passage, to South river. The other vessels, with soldiers and a few settlers, also soon arrived.

It is said that at this time the "public," exercises of religion were not allowed to any sects in Holland except the Calvinists. But all others were permitted to engage freely in their worship in private houses, which were in fact, as if public, these places of preaching being spacious and of sufficient size for any assembly. Under this construction of the law every religion was in fact tolerated.*

The Lutherans in Holland sent a clergyman, Ernestus Goetwater, to New Amsterdam, to organize a church. The Directors wrote, " It is our intention to permit every one to have freedom within his own dwelling, to serve God in such manner as his religion requires, but without authorizing any public meetings or conventicles."

This tolerance, so imperfect in the light of the nineteenth century, was very noble in the dark days of the seventeenth. Upon the arrival of Goetwater at New Amsterdam, the clergy of the Reformed church remonstrated against his being permitted to preach. The governor, adhering to his policy of bigotry, forbade him to hold any meeting, or to do any clerical service, but to regulate his conduct according to the placards of the province against private conventicles. Soon after this the governor ordered him to leave the colony and to return to Holland. This harsh decree was however suspended out of regard to the feeble health of Goetwater.

On the 6th of August, 1657, a ship arrived at

* History of New Netherland by E. B. O'Callaghan, Vol 2. p. 317

New Amsterdam with several Quakers on board.
Two of them, women, began to preach publicly in
the streets. They were arrested and imprisoned.
Soon after they were discharged and embarked on
board a ship to sail through Hell Gate, to Rhode Isl-
and, "where," writes Domine Megapolensis, "all
kinds of scum dwell, for it is nothing else than a
sink for New England."

One of the Quakers, Robert Hodgson, went
over to Long Island. At Hempstead he was arrested and committed to prison, and was thence transferred to one of the dungeons of fort Amsterdam.
He was brought before the Council, convicted of the
crime of preaching contrary to the law, and was sentenced to pay a fine of six hundred guilders, about
two hundred and forty dollars, or to labor two years
at a wheelbarrow, with a negro.

After a few days' imprisonment he was chained
to the wheelbarrow and commanded to work. He
refused. A negro was ordered to beat him with a
tarred rope, which he did until the sufferer fell, in
utter exhaustion, almost senseless to the ground.
The story of the persecutions which this unhappy
man endured, is almost too dreadful to be told.
But it ought to be told as a warning against all religious intolerance.

"Not satisfied," writes O'Callaghan, " his perse

cutors had him lifted up. The negro again beat him until he fell a second time, after receiving, as was estimated, one hundred blows. Notwithstand-ing all this, he was kept, in the heat of the sun, chained to the wheelbarrow, his body bruised and swollen, faint from want of food, until at length he could no longer support himself and he was obliged to sit down.

" The night found him again in his cell, and the morrow at the wheelbarrow, with a sentinel over him, to prevent all conversation. On the third day he was again led forth, chained as before. He still refused to work, for he " had committed no evil." He was then led anew before the director-general, who ordered him to work, otherwise he should be whipt every day. He was again chained to the barrow and threatened, if he should speak to any person, with more severe punishment. But not be-ing able to keep him silent, he was taken back to his dungeon, where he was kept several days, " two nights and one day and a half of which without bread or water."

" The rage of persecution was still unsatiated. He was now removed to a private room, stripped to his waist, and then hung up to the ceiling by his hands, with a heavy log of wood tied to his feet, so that he could not turn his body. A strong negro then commenced lashing him with rods until his flesh was cut in pieces. Now let down, he was thrown again into his loathsome dungeon, where he was kept ten days, in solitary confinement, after which he was brought forth to undergo a repetition of the same barbarous torture. He was now kept like a slave to hard work."

His case eventually excited so much compassion that Stuyvesant's sister interfered, and implored her brother so importunately that he was at last induced to liberate the unfortunate man. Let a firm Quaker resolve that he will not do something, and let a Governor Stuyvesant resolve that he shall do it, and it is indeed " Greek meeting Greek."

Henry Townsend, of Jamaica, ventured to hold prayer-meetings in his house, in defiance of the ordinance against conventicles. The governor sen- tenced him to pay a fine of eight pounds and to leave the province within six weeks, under pain of corporeal punishment. This sentence was followed by a proclamation, fining any one fifty pounds who should entertain a Quaker for a single night, and confiscating any vessels which should bring a Quaker to the province.

The inhabitants of Flushing, where Townsend had formerly resided, and where he was very highly respected, issued a noble remonstrance to Governor

Stuyvesant against this persecution of their former townsman.

The remonstrance was drawn up by the town clerk, Edward Hart, and was signed by all the adult male inhabitants, twenty-nine in number. The memorial said :

"We are commanded by the law of God to do good unto all men. The law of love, peace and liberty, extending in the state to Jews, Turks and Egyptians, forms the glory of Holland. So love, peace and liberty extending to all in Christ Jesus, condemn hatred, war and bondage. We desire not to offend one of Christ's little ones under whatever form, name or title he may appear, whether Presbyterian, Independent, Baptist or Quaker. On the contrary we desire to do to all as we could wish all to do to us. Should any of those people come in love among us, we cannot lay violent hands upon them. We must give them free ingress and egress into our houses."

This remonstrance was carried to New Amsterdam by Tobias Feake, and presented to the governor. His indignation was roused. Feake was arrested and committed to prison. The sheriff was sent to Flushing to bring Hart and two of the magistrates, Farrington and Noble, to the presence of the enraged governor. It was a fearful thing to fall into

o*

his hands when his wrath was inflamed. They were imprisoned for some time, and were then released upon their humbly imploring the pardon of the governor, expressing their deep regret that they had signed the remonstrance and promising that they would sin in that way, no more. The town itself was punished by the prohibition in future of all town meetings, without the permission of the governor. Indeed the mass of the settlers were no longer to decide upon their local affairs, but a committee of seven persons was to decide all such questions. All who were dissatisfied with these arrangements were ordered to sell their property and leave the town.

It is not necessary to continue the record of this disgraceful persecution. The governor was unrelenting. Whoever ventured to oppose his will felt the weight of his chastising hand.

New Amsterdam consisted of wooden houses clustered together. The danger from fire was very great. The governor imposed a tax of a beaver skin, or its equivalent upon each householder to pay for two hundred and fifty leather fire buckets and hooks and ladders, to be procured in Holland. He also established a "rattle watch" to traverse the streets from nine o'clock in the evening until morning drum-beat.

Stuyvesant would allow nothing to be done

which he did not control. The education of the young was greatly neglected. Jacob Corlaer opened a school. The governor peremptorily closed it, because he had presumed to take the office without governmental permission. To establish a place of amusement the governor formed a village called Haarlem, at the northern extremity of Manhattan island. He also constructed a good road over the island, through the forest, " so that it may be made easy to come hither, and return to that village on horseback or in a wagon." A ferry was also established to Long Island.

Staten Island was a dreary waste. It had not recovered from the massacre of 1655. Efforts were made to encourage the former settlers to return to their desolated homes, and to encourage fresh colonists to take up their residence upon the island. To promote the settlement of the west side of the North river, Stuyvesant purchased from the Indians, all the territory now known as Bergen, in New Jersey.

This purchase comprised the extensive region, " beginning from the great rock above Wiehackan, and from there right through the land, until above the island Sikakes, and from there to the Kill van Col, and so along to the Constables Hook, and thence again to the rock above Wiehackan."

The settlement at Esopus, was in many respects in a flourishing condition.   But it was so much more convenient for the farmers to have their dwellings in the midst of the fields they cultivated, instead of clustering them together in a compact village, that they persisted in the dangerous practice, notwithstanding all the warnings of the governor.   There were individuals also who could not be restrained from paying brandy to the savages for their peltries The intoxicated Indians often committed outrages. One of the settlers was killed.   The house and out-buildings of another were burned.   The Dutch retaliated by destroying the cornfields of the Indians, hoping thus to drive them to a distance.   At this time, in May, 1658, there were about seventy colonists at Esopus.   They had widely extended fields of grain.   But the Indians were becoming daily more inimical, and the alarmed colonists wrote to Governor Stuyvesant, saying,

"We pray you to send forty or fifty soldiers to save Esopus, which, if well settled, might supply the whole of New Netherland with provisions."

The governor ordered a redoubt to be built at Esopus, sent an additional supply of ammunition, and taking fifty soldiers with him, went up the river to ascertain, by a personal investigation, the wants of the people.   He urged them strenuously to unite in a village, which could be easily palisaded, and which would thus afford them complete protection. The colonists objected that it would be very difficult to remove from their farms, while their crops were ungathered, and that it would be impossible to select a site for the village which would please all. The governor refused to leave the soldiers with them unless they would immediately decide to concentrate in a village. In that case he would remain and aid them in constructing the palisade till it should be completed.

In the mean time messengers were sent to all the neighboring chiefs inviting them to come to Esopus to meet "the grand sachem from Manhattan." Sixty of these plumed warriors were soon assembled, with a few women and children. The governor, with two followers and an interpreter, met them beneath the widespread branches of an aged tree. One of the chiefs opened the interview by a long speech, in which he recounted all the injuries which he conceived that the Indians had experienced from the foreigners. The governor listened patiently. He then replied,

" These events occurred, as you well know, before my time. I am not responsible for them. Has any injury been done you since I came into the country? Your chiefs have asked us, over and over again, to

make a settlement among them. We have not had
a foot of your land without paying for it. We do
not desire to have any more without making you
full compensation. Why then have you committed
this murder, burned our houses and killed our cattle? And why do you continue to threaten our
people?"

There was a long pause, as though the chiefs
were meditating upon the answer which should be
made. Then one of them rose and, with great deliberation and dignity of manner, said,

"You Swannekins," for that was the name they
gave the Dutchmen, "have sold our children drink.
We cannot then control them, or prevent them from
fighting. This murder has not been committed by
any of our tribe, but by a Minnisinck, who now skulks
among the Haverstraws. 'Twas he who fired the two
houses and then fled. We have no malice. We do
not wish to fight. But we cannot control our young
men after you have sold them drink."

The best of the argument thus far, was manifestly with the Indians. The irascible governor lost
his temper. "If any of your young savages," said
he, "want to fight, let them come on. I will place
man against man. Nay, I will place twenty against
forty of your hotheads. It is not manly to threaten
farmers and women and children who are not war-

riors. If this be not stopped I shall be compelled
to retaliate on old and young, women and children.
I expect of you that you will repair all damages and
seize the murderer if he come among you.

"The Dutch are now to live together in one
spot. It is desirable that you should sell us the
whole of the Esopus land and move farther into the
interior. It is not well for you to reside so near the
Swannekins. Their cattle may eat your corn and
thus cause fresh disturbance."

The Council was closed with professions of friendship on both sides. The Indians promised to take
the suggestions of the governor into careful consideration. The settlers also decided to adopt the
counsel of the governor. They agreed unanimously to form themselves into a village, leaving it with
Governor Stuyvesant to select the site. He chose
a spot at the bend of the creek, where three sides
would be surrounded by water. Two hundred and
ten yards of palisades formed the sufficient enclosure.

All hands now went to work energetically.
While thus employed a band of Indian warriors, in
their most showy attire, was seen approaching. It
was feared that they were on the war path, and the
soldiers immediately stood to their arms. It is undeniable that the Indians seemed ever disposed to
cherish kindly feelings when justly treated.

These kind hearted savages fifty in number, not-withstanding all the wrongs which they had endured, came forward and one of them, addressing the governor, said,

In token of our good will, and that we have laid aside all malice, we request the Grand Sachem to accept as a free present, the land on which he has commenced his settlement. We give it to grease his feet, as he has undertaken so long and painful a journey to visit us."

The labor of three weeks completed the defences. The buildings were reared within the enclosure. A strong guard-house, sixteen feet by twenty-three, was built in the northeast corner of the village. A bridge was thrown across the creek, and temporary quarters were erected for the soldiers. The energetic governor having accomplished all this in a month, left twenty-four soldiers behind him to guard the village, and returned to Manhattan.

In 1658, the little settlement of New Amstel presented quite a flourishing appearance. It had become a goodly town of about one hundred houses," containing about five hundred inhabitants. As many of these were Waldenses, Swedes and emigrants from other nationalities, they seemed to think themselves independent of the provincial authorities at

New Amsterdam. The governor therefore visited the place in person, and called upon all to take the oath of allegiance.

There was great jealousy felt by the governor in reference to the encroachments of the English. They were pressing their claims everywhere. They were establishing small settlements upon territory undeniably belonging to the Dutch. English emigrants were crowding the Dutch colonies and were daily gaining in influence. Though they readily took the oath of allegiance to the Dutch authorities, all their sympathies were with England and the English colonies.

The Directors of the Company wrote to Stuyvesant recommending him "to disentangle himself in the best manner possible from the Englishmen whom he had allowed to settle at New Amstel. And at all events not to admit any English besides them in that vicinity, much less to allure them by any means whatever."

There were many indications that the English were contemplating pressing up from Virginia to the beautiful region of the Delaware. The Directors urged Stuyvesant to purchase immediately from the Indians the tract of land between Cape Henlopen and Bombay Hook. This contained a frontage on Delaware bay of about seventy miles.

"You will perceive," they wrote, "that speed is
required, if for nothing else, that we may prevent
other nations, and principally our English neighbors,
as we really apprehend that this identical spot has
attracted their notice. When we reflect upon the
insufferable proceedings of that nation not only by
intruding themselves upon our possessions about the
North, to which our title is indisputable, and when
we consider the bold arrogance and faithlessness of
those who are residing within our jurisdiction, we
cannot expect any good from that quarter."

In the autumn of this year a very momentous
event occurred. Though it was but the death of
a single individual, that individual was Oliver Cromwell. Under his powerful sway England had risen
to a position of dignity and power such as the nation
had never before attained. A terrible storm swept
earth and sky during the night in which his tempest-
uous earthly life came to a close. The roar of the
hurricane appalled all minds, as amid floods of rain
trees were torn up by the roots, and houses were
unroofed. The friends of the renowned Protector
said that nature was weeping and mourning in her
loudest accents over the great loss humanity was
experiencing in the death of its most illustrious
benefactor. The enemies of Cromwell affirmed that
the Prince of the Power of the Air had come with

all his shrieking demons, to seize the soul of the dying and bear it to its merited doom.

Scarce six months passed away ere the reins of government fell from the feeble hands of Richard, the eldest son and heir of Oliver Cromwell, and Monk marched across the Tweed and paved the way for the restoration of Charles the Second.

To add to the alarm of the Dutch, Massachusetts, taking the ground that the boundary established by the treaty of Hartford, extended only "so far as New Haven had jurisdiction," claimed by virtue of royal grant all of the land north of the forty-second degree of latitude to the Merrimac river, and extending from the Atlantic to the Pacific ocean. The forty-second parallel of latitude crossed the Hudson near Red Hook and Saugerties. This boundary line transferred the whole of the upper Hudson and at least four-fifths of the State of New York to Massachusetts.

In accordance with this claim, Massachusetts granted a large section of land on the east side of the Hudson river, opposite the present site of Albany, to a number of her principal merchants to open energetically a trade with the Indians for their furs. An exploring party was also sent from Hartford to sail up the North river and examine its shores in reference to future settlements. The

English could not enter the Hudson and pass fort Amsterdam with their vessels without permission of the Dutch. This permission Stuyvesant persistently refused.

"The Dutch," said the inflexible governor, "never have forbidden the natives to trade with other nations. They prohibit such trade only on their own streams and purchased lands. They cannot grant Massachusetts or any other government any title to such privilege or a free passage through their rivers, without the surrender of their honor, reputation, property and blood, their bodies and lives."

CHAPTER X.

The Esopus War.

THE exploring party from Massachusetts, which had ascended the North river, found a region around the Wappinger Kill, a few miles below the present site of Poughkeepsie, which they pronounced to be more beautiful than any spot which they had seen in New England. Here they decided to establish their settlement. Stuyvesant, informed of this, resolved to anticipate them. He wrote immediately to Holland urging the Company to send out at once as many Polish, Lithuanian, Prussian, Dutch and Flemish peasants as possible, " to form a colony there."

It would seem that no experience, however dreadful, could dissuade individuals of the Dutch colonists from supplying the natives with brandy. At Esopus, in August, 1659, a man by the name of Thomas Chambers employed eight Indians to assist him in husking corn. At the end of their day's work he insanely supplied them with brandy. This led to a midnight carouse in which the poor savages, bereft of reason, howled and shrieked and fired their muskets, though without getting into any quarrel among themselves.

The uproar alarmed the garrison in the blockhouse. The sergeant of the guard was sent out, with a few soldiers, to ascertain the cause of the disorder. He returned with the report that it was only the revelry of a band of drunken savages.

One of the soldiers in the fort, Jansen Stot, called upon some of his comrades to follow him. Ensign Smith, who was in command, forbade them to go. In defiance of his orders they left the fort, and creeping through the underbrush, wantonly took deliberate aim, discharged a volley of bullets upon the inebriated savages, who were harming nobody but themselves. One was killed outright. Others were severely wounded. The soldiers, having performed this insane act, retreated, with the utmost speed to the fort. There never has been any denial that such were the facts in the case. They help to corroborate the remark of Mr. Moulton that "the cruelty of the Indians towards the whites will, when traced, be discovered, in almost every case, to have been provoked by oppression or aggression."

Ensign Smith, finding that he could no longer control his soldiers, indignantly resolved to return down the river to New Amsterdam. The inhabitants of Esopus were greatly alarmed. It was well known that the savages would not allow such an outrage to pass unavenged. The withdrawal of the soldiers would leave them at the mercy of those so justly exasperated. To prevent this the people hired every boat in the neighborhood. Ensign Smith then decided to send an express by land, to inform Governor Stuyvesant of the alarming state of affairs and to solicit his immediate presence.

A party of soldiers was sent to escort the express a few miles down the river banks. As these soldiers were returning, they fell into an ambuscade of the Indians, and thirteen of them were taken prisoners. War, horrible war, was now declared. The war-whoop resounded around the stockade at Esopus from five hundred savage throats. Every house, barn and corn-stack within their reach was burned. Cattle and horses were killed. The fort was so closely invested day and night that not a colonist could step outside of the stockade. The Indians, foiled in all their attempts to set fire to the fortress,

burnt ten of their prisoners at the stake. For three
weeks this fierce warfare continued without interruption.

When the tidings of this new war, caused by so
dastardly an outrage, reached Manhattan, it created
a terrible panic. It could not be doubted that all
the Indians would sympathize with their outraged
brethren. The farmers, apprehending immediate
attack, fled from all directions, with their families, to
the fort, abandoning their homes, grain and cattle.
Even many villages on Long Island were utterly
deserted.

The administrative energies of Governor Stuyvesant were remarkably developed on this occasion.
In the following terms, Mr. O'Callaghan, in his
admirable history of New Netherland, describes the
difficulties he encountered and his mode of sur-
mounting them:

"Governor Stuyvesant, though laboring under
severe indisposition, visited in person all the adjoining villages, encouraging the well-disposed, stimulat-
ing the timid and urging the farmers everywhere to
fortify and defend their villages. He summoned
next the burgomasters, schepens,* and officers of
the militia of New Amsterdam, and laid before them
the distressing situation of Esopus. They proposed

* Officers of a very important muni ipal court.

to enlist by beat of drum, a sufficient number of men, and to encourage volunteers by resolving that whatever savages might be captured should be declared 'good prizes.'

"Stuyvesant, however, was opposed to this mode of proceeding. It would cause, in his opinion, too great a delay, as those at Esopus were already besieged some nine or ten days. He was left, notwithstanding, in a minority. Two more days were thus irretrievably lost; for at the end of that time only six or eight had enlisted, 'such a terrible horror had overpowered the citizens.'

"Captain Newton and Lieutenant Stillwell were now dispatched to all the English and Dutch villages, and letters were addressed to fort Orange and Rensselaerswyck, ordering out the Company's servants, calling for volunteers and authorizing the raising of a troop of mounted rangers. The half-dozen servants in fort Amsterdam, every person belonging to the artillery, all the clerks in the public offices, four of the Director-General's servants, three of the hands belonging to his brewery and five or six new comers, were put under requisition.

Nothing could overcome the reluctance of the burghers. The one disheartened the other; the more violent maintaining that they were obliged to defend only their own homes, and that no citizen

10

could be forced to jeopardize his life in fighting barbarous savages.

"Discouraged and almost deprived of hope by
this opposition, the Director-General again summoned the city magistrates. He informed them that
he had now some forty men, and that he expected
between twenty and thirty Englishmen from the
adjoining villages. He therefore ordered that the
three companies of the city militia be paraded next
day in his presence, armed and equipped, in order
that one last effort might be made to obtain volunteers. If he should then fail of success, he announced his intention to make a draft.

"The companies paraded before the fort on the
following morning according to orders. Stuyvesant
addressed them in most exciting terms. He ap-
pealed to their sense both of honor and of duty, and
represented to them how ardently they would look
for aid, if they unfortunately were placed in a situation similar to that in which their brethren of Esopus
now found themselves. He concluded his harangue
by calling upon all such as would accompany him
either for pay or as volunteers, to step forward to
the rescue.

"Few came forward, only twenty-four or twenty-
five persons. This number being considered insuffi-
cient, lots were immediately ordered to be drawn by

one of the companies and those on whom they fell were warned to be ready on the next Sunday, on pain of paying fifty guilders. 'However,' said the governor, 'if any person is weak-hearted or discouraged he may procure a substitute provided he declares himself instantaneously.' "

In this way the governor raised a force of one hundred and eighty men. Of this number one hundred were drafted men, sixty-five volunteers, twenty-five of whom were Englishmen, and there were also twenty friendly Indians from Long Island.

With this force the governor embarked on Sunday evening, October 10th, after the second sermon, for the rescue of Esopus. Upon his arrival at that place he found that the savages, unable to penetrate the fort, had raised the siege and retired beyond the possibility of pursuit. They had doubtless watched the river with their scouts, who informed them of the approach of the troops. The governor, leaving a sufficient force to protect the village, returned with the remainder of the expedition to Manhattan.

During the siege the loss of the Dutch was one man killed and five or six wounded. The Indians also succeeded, by means of burning arrows, in firing one dwelling house and several stacks of corn within the palisades. As the troops were re-embarking the governor witnessed an occurrence which he declares "he blushes to mention." As all the troops could not go on board at once, a portion waited until the first division had embarked. Some of the sentinels hearing a dog bark, fired one or two shots. This created a terrible panic. The citizens, whose ears had been pierced by the shrieks of their countrymen, whom the Indians had tortured at the stake, were so terror-stricken that they lost all self-possession. "Many of them threw themselves into the water before they had seen an enemy."

The most friendly relations existed between the Mohawks and the settlers in the vicinity of Albany. A very extensive trade, equally lucrative to both parties, was there in operation. The Indians, being treated justly, were as harmless as lambs. When they heard of the troubles at Esopus they declared that they would take no part in the war. They could not but feel that the Indians had been deeply outraged. But with unexpected intelligence they decided that they would not retaliate by wreaking vengeance upon their long-tried friends. To confirm their friendly alliance, the authorities at fort Orange sent an embassy of twenty-five of their principal inhabitants to the Indian settlement at Caughnawaga. This was about forty miles west of Albany on the north bank of the Mohawk river and near the site of the present shire town of Montgomery county.

A large number of chiefs, from all the neighboring villages, attended. The council fire was lighted, and the calumet of peace was smoked. One of the Dutch delegation thus addressed the assembly!

"Brothers, sixteen years have now passed away, since friendship and fraternity were first established between you and the Hollanders. Since then we have been bound to each other by an iron chain. That chain has never been broken by us or by you. We hope that the Mohawks will remain our brothers for all time.

"Our chiefs are very angry that the Dutch will sell brandy to your people. They have always forbidden them to do so. Forbid your people also. Eighteen days ago you asked us not to sell any brandy to your people. Brothers, if your people do not come to buy brandy of us, we shall not sell any to them. Two days ago twenty or thirty kegs came to us, all to be filled with brandy. Are you willing that we should take from your people their brandy and their kegs. If so, say this before all here present."

With this speech there was presented to the chiefs several bundles of wampum, seventy pounds of powder, a hundred pounds of lead, fifteen axes

two beavers worth of knives. The chiefs were
highly pleased with the presents and eagerly gave
their consent that the Dutch should seize the liquor
kegs of the Indians.

The authorities at fort Orange, having secured
the friendship of the Mohawks, endeavored to obtain
an armistice with the Indians at Esopus, and a release of the captives they had taken. Several Mohawk and Mohegan chiefs, as mediators, visited
Esopus, on this mission of mercy. They were par-
tially successful. An armistice was reluctantly assented to, and two captives were liberated. The
Indians, however, still retained a number of children, they having killed all the adults. Those who
had agreed to the armistice were not the principal
chiefs, and the spirit of the war remained unbroken.

Under these circumstances Stuyvesant wrote to
Holland for aid. In his letter he said, " If a farmer
cannot plough, sow or reap, in a newly settled
country, without being harassed ; if the citizens and
merchants cannot freely navigate the streams and
rivers, they will doubtless leave the country and
seek a residence in some place where they can find
a government to protect them."

The Directors wrote back urging him to employ
the Mohawks and other friendly tribes against the
Esopus Indians   The governor replied,

"The Mohawks are, above all other savages, a vain-glorious, proud and bold tribe. If their aid be demanded and obtained, and success follow, they will only become the more inflated, and we the more contemptible in the eyes of the other tribes. If we did not then reward their services, in a manner satisfactory to their greedy appetites, they would incessantly revile us, and were this retorted, it might lead to collision. It is therefore safer to stand on our own feet as long as possible."

The governor had a long controversy with the Massachusetts authorities in reference to its claim to the upper valley of the Hudson. In this he expressed very strongly the title of Holland to the North river.

"Printed histories," he writes, "archives, journals, and registers prove that the North river of New Netherland was discovered in the year 1609, by Hendrick Hudson, captain of the Half Moon, in the service and at the expense of the Dutch East India Company. Upon the report of the captain several merchants of Amsterdam sent another ship, in the following year, up the said river. These merchants obtained from the States-General a charter to navigate the same. For their security they erected in 1614, a fort on Castle Island, near fort Orange.

New Netherland, including the North river, was afterwards offered to the West India Company, who,
in the year 1624, two years before Charles I. ascended the throne of England, actually and effectually possessed and fortified the country and planted
colonies therein. The assertion that the Hudson
river is within the Massachusetts patent granted but
thirty-two years ago, therefore, scarcely deserves a
serious answer."

Notwithstanding the undeniable strength of his
argument, Governor Stuyvesant felt very uneasy.
To his friends he said,

"The power of New England overbalances ours
tenfold. To protest against their usurpations would
be folly. They would only laugh at us."

As hostilities still continued with the Esopus
Indians, Governor Stuyvesant again visited that post,
hoping to obtain an interview with the chiefs, and
to arrange a peace. Ensign Smith, with a very
strong party of forty men, had utterly routed and
put to flight two bands of Indians, one containing
fifty warriors, the other one hundred. He took
twelve warriors prisoners. They were sent to fort
Amsterdam. In the mean time Stuyvesant had
succeeded in renewing a treaty of alliance with the
Indian tribes on Long Island, Staten Island, and at
Hackensack, Haverstraw and Weckquaesgeek. The

Long Island Indians consented to send some of their children to fort Amsterdam to be educated.

The Esopus Indians were now left in a very deplorable condition. Their brethren, on the upper Hudson, had refused to co-operate with them. Their routed bands were being driven across the mountains and many of their warriors were captives. To use the contemptuous language of the times, "they did nothing now but bawl for peace, peace."

There had never been a more favorable opportunity to secure a lasting peace, and to win back the affections of the Indians. By universal admission the colonists were outrageously in the wrong in provoking the conflict. They had given the Indians brandy until they had become intoxicated. And then half a dozen drunken soldiers had discharged a volley of bullets upon them as they were revelling in noisy but harmless orgies.

Had the governor frankly acknowledged that the colonists were in the wrong; had he made full amends, according to the Indian custom, for the great injury inflicted upon them, they would have been more than satisfied. Even more friendly relations than had ever before existed might have been established.

But instead of this the governor assumed that the Indians were entirely in the wrong; that they

10*

had wantonly commenced a series of murders and
burnings without any provocation. The Esopus
chiefs were afraid to meet the angry governor with
proposals for peace. They therefore employed three
Mohegan chiefs as their mediators. They offered
to cease all hostilities, to abandon the Esopus country entirely, and surrender it to the Dutch if the
Indian captives, whom the Dutch held, might be restored to them. These very honorable proposals
were rejected. The Mohegan chiefs were told that
the governor could not enter into any treaty of
peace with the Esopus Indians unless their own
chiefs came to fort Amsterdam to hold a council.
And immediately the Indian captives received the
awful doom of consignment to life-long slavery with
the negroes, upon a tropical island, which was but
a glowing sandbank in the Caribbean sea.

"On the next day," writes Mr. O'Callaghan, "an
order was issued, banishing the Esopus savages, some
fifteen or twenty, to the insalubrious climate of
Curaçoa, to be employed there or at Buenaire with
the negroes in the Company's service. Two or three
others were retained at fort Amsterdam to be pun
ished as it should be thought proper. By this harsh
policy Stuyvesant laid the foundations of another
Esopus war, for the Indians never forgot their
banished brethren."

It was ascertained that several miles up the Esopus creek the Indians were planting corn. It was the 20th of May, 1660. Ensign Smith took a party of seventy-five men and advanced upon them. The barking of dogs announced his approach just as his band arrived within sight of the wigwams. They all made good their retreat with the exception of one, the oldest and best of their chiefs. His name was Preumaker. We know not whether pride of character or infirmity prevented his escape. It is said, however, that he received the soldiers very haughtily, aiming his gun at them and saying, "What are you doing here, you dogs?"

The weapon was easily wrenched from his feeble hands. A consultation was held as to what should be done with the courageous but powerless old chief. "As it was a considerable distance to carry him," writes Ensign Smith, "we struck him down with his own axe."

At length the sufferings of the Esopus Indians became so great from the burning of the villages and the trampling down of their cornfields, the loss of their armies and the terrified flight of their starving women and children, that they were constrained to make another effort for peace.

On the 11th of July, Governor Stuyvesant left New Amsterdam for Esopus. Messengers were dispatched to summon the Esopus chiefs to his presence. Appalled by the fate of their brethren, who had been sent as slaves to the West Indies, they were afraid to come. After waiting several days the governor sent envoys to the chiefs of other tribes, urging them " to bring the Esopus savages to terms."

At length four Esopus chiefs appeared before the gate of the village. Delegates from other tribes also appeared, and a grand council was held. It is very evident from this interview, that many of the more delicate feelings of the civilized man had full sway in the hearts of these poor Indians. Instead of imploring peace themselves, the Esopus Indians employed two chiefs, one of the Mohawk and the other of the Mingua tribe, to make the proposition in their behalf.

Governor Stuyvesant assented to peace upon condition that the Mohawks and the Minguas would stand as security for the faithful observance of the terms exacted. The chiefs of these tribes agreeing to this, in a formal speech admonished the Esopus chiefs to live with the Dutch as brothers. And then, turning to the Dutch, in a speech equally impressive, they warned them not to irritate the Indians by unjust treatment. The Indians were compelled to yield to such terms as Stuyvesant proposed.

All the lands of Esopus were surrendered to the Dutch. The starving Indians were to receive eight hundred schepels of corn as ransom for the captive christians. The Indian warriors sent as slaves to the West Indies, were to be left to their awful fate. The mediators were held responsible for the faithful execution of the treaty. Should the Esopus Indians break it, the mediators were bound to assist the Dutch in punishing them. No spirituous liquors were to be *drank* near the houses of the Dutch. No *armed* Indians to approach a Dutch plantation. Murderers were to be mutually surrendered, and damages reciprocally paid for.

Thus were the Esopus Indians driven from their homes, deprived of their independence and virtually ruined. Having thus triumphantly though cruelly settled this difficulty, Stuyvesant went up to fort Orange, where he held another grand council with the chiefs of all the tribes in those regions.

A clergyman was sent to Esopus and a church organized of sixteen members. In September, 1660, Domine Selyus was installed as the clergyman of Brooklyn, where he found one elder, two deacons and twenty-four church members. There were, at that time thirty-one families in Brooklyn, containing a population of one hundred and thirty-four persons. They had no church but worshipped in a barn. Governor Stuyvesant contributed nearly eighty dollars annually to the support of this minister, but upon condition that he should preach every Sunday afternoon, at his farm or bouwery upon Manhattan Island.

The last of May, Charles the Second, the fugitive King of England, was returning from his wanderings on the continent to ascend the throne of his ancestors. He was a weak man, of imperturbable good nature. On his way to London he stopped at the Hague, where he was magnificently entertained. In taking leave of the States-General he was lavish of his expressions of friendship. He declared that he should feel jealous should the Dutch prefer the friendship of any other state to that of Great Britain.

At that time Holland was in commercial enterprise, the most prosperous nation upon the globe; decidedly in advance of England. The British parliament envied Holland her commercial supremacy. "The Convention Parliament," writes Mr. Brodhead, "which had called home the king, took early steps to render still more obnoxious one of England's most selfish measures. The Navigation Act of 1651 was revised; and it was now enacted that after the first day of December, 1660, no merchandise should be imported into, or exported from any of his majesty's plantations or territories in Asia, Africa or America, except in English vessels of which the master and three-fourths of the mariners at least are English."

Immediately after this, Lord Baltimore demanded the surrender of New Amstel and all the lands on the west side of Delaware bay. "All the country," it was said by his envoy, "up to the fortieth degree, was granted to Lord Baltimore. The grant has been confirmed by the king and sanctioned by parliament. You are weak, we are strong, you had better yield at once."

A very earnest and prolonged discussion ensued. The Dutch Company said, "We hold our rights by the States-General. We are resolved to defend those rights. If Lord Baltimore will persevere and resort to violent measures, we shall use all the means which God and nature have given us to protect the inhabitants and preserve their possessions."

This was indeed an alarming state of affairs for New Amstel. Various disasters had befallen the colony, so that it now numbered but thirty families. The garrison had been reduced, by desertion, to twenty-five men ; and of these but eight or ten were in the principal fort. The English were in such strength upon the Chesapeake, that they could easily send five hundred men to the Delaware. Very earnest diplomatic intercourse was opened between

the States-General and the British Parliament upon
these questions.

Governor Stuyvesant, whose attention had been
somewhat engrossed by the Indian difficulties, now
renewed his persecution of the Quakers. Notwithstanding the law against private conventicles, Henry
Townsend at Rustdorp, who had been already twice
fined, persisted in holding private meetings in his
house. He was arrested with two others, and carried to fort Amsterdam. Townsend and Tilton
were banished from the colony. Two magistrates
were appointed as spies to inform of any future
meetings, and some soldiers were stationed in the
village to suppress them. Whatever Governor Stuyvesant undertook to do he accomplished very thoroughly. The following paper was drawn up which
the inhabitants were required to sign:

"If any meetings or conventicles of Quakers
shall be held in this town of Rustdorp, that we
know of, we will give information to the authority
set up by the governor, and we will also give the
authorities of the town such assistance against any
such persons as needs may require."

A few refused to sign this paper. They were
punished by having the soldiers quartered upon
them.

Fort Orange was, at this time, the extreme frontier post, in the north and west of New Netherland. Though the country along the Mohawk river had been explored for a considerable distance, there were no settlements there, though one or two huts had been reared in the vicinity of the Cohoes Falls. This whole region had abounded with beavers and wild deer. But the fur trade had been pushed with so much vigor that the country was now almost entirely destitute of peltries. The colonists wished to purchase the fertile lands in the valley of the Mohawk, and the Indians manifested a willingness to sell them.

CHAPTER XI.

The Disastrous Year.

IN the year 1661, the Company purchased of
Melyn, the patroon, for about five hundred dollars,
all his rights to lands on Staten Island. Thus the
whole island became the property of the Company.
Grants of lands were immediately issued to individuals. The Waldenses, and the Huguenots from
Rochelle in France, were invited to settle upon the
island. A block-house was built which was armed
with two cannon and garrisoned by ten soldiers.
Fourteen families were soon gathered in a little
settlement south of the Narrows.

Upon the restoration of Charles the Second, in
England, the Royalists and churchmen insisted upon
the restoration of the hierarchy. The Restoration

was far from being the unanimous act of the nation.
The republicans and dissenters, disappointed and
persecuted, were disposed in ever increasing numbers, to take refuge in the New World. The West
India Company of Holland being in possession of
a vast territory, between the Hudson and the Delaware, which was quite uninhabited, save by a few
tribes of Indians, availed themselves of this opportunity to endeavor to draw emigrants from all parts
of Europe, and especially from England, to form
settlements upon their lands.

They issued proclamations inviting settlers and
offering them large inducements. The country,
which embraced mainly what is now New Jersey,
was described in glowing terms as if it were a second
Eden. And yet there was no gross exaggeration in
the narrative.

"This land," they wrote, "is but six weeks' sail
from Holland. It is fertile in the extreme. The
climate serene and temperate, is the best in the
world. The soil is ready for the plough, and seed
can be committed to it with scarcely any preparation. The most valuable timber is abundant. The
forest presents in profusion, nuts and wild fruit of
every description. The richest furs can be obtained
without trouble. Deer, turkeys, pigeons and almost
every variety of wild game, are found in the woods.

And there is every encouragement for the establishment of fisheries."

Having presented this view of the region, to
which emigrants were invited, and having also announced an exceedingly attractive charter of civil
and religious privileges which would be granted
them, in the following terms the invitation to emi-
grate was urged:

"Therefore if any of the good christians, who
may be assured of the advantages to mankind of
plantations in these latitudes, shall be disposed to
transport themselves to said place, they shall have
full liberty to live in the fear of the Lord upon the
aforesaid good conditions and shall be likewise
courteously used.

"We grant to all christian people of tender conscience, in England or elsewhere oppressed, full
liberty to erect a colony between New England and
Virginia in America, now within the jurisdiction of
Peter Stuyvesant."

Twenty-three families, most of them French,
established a settlement on Long Island, at the place
now called Bushwick. The village grew rapidly and
in two years had forty men able to bear arms.

The proclamation issued by the Company, inviting emigrants to settle upon the lands between
the Hudson and the Delaware, attracted much

attention in Europe. Committees were sent to examine the lands which it was proposed thus to colonize. The region between New Amstel and Cape Henlopen, being quite unoccupied, attracted much attention. A company, the members of which may be truly called a peculiar people, decided to settle there. An extraordinary document was drawn up, consisting of one hundred and seventeen articles for the government of the association. In this singular agreement it is written:

"The associates are to be either married men or single men twenty-four years old, who are free from debt. Each one is bound to obey the ordinances of the society and not to seek his own advancement over any other member. No clergyman is to be admitted into the society. Religious services are to be as simple as possible. Every Sunday and holiday the people are to assemble, sing a Psalm and listen to a chapter from the Bible, to be read by one of the members in rotation. After this another Psalm is to be sung. At the end of these exercises the court shall be opened for public business. The object of the association being to establish a harmonious society of persons of different religious sentiments, all intractable people shall be excluded from it, such as those in communion with the Roman See, usurious Jews, English stiff-necked Quakers, Puritans, fool-hardy believers in the Millenium and obstinate modern pretenders to revelation."

While the Company in Holland, were inviting emigrants to their territory of the New World, with the fullest promises of religious toleration, their governor, Stuyvesant, was unrelentingly persecuting all who did not sustain the established religion.

A very quiet, thoughtful, inoffensive man, John Brown, an Englishman, moved from Boston to Flushing. He was a plain farmer, very retiring in his habits and a man of but few words. From curiosity he attended a Quaker meeting. His meditative spirit was peculiarly impressed with the simplicity of their worship. He invited them to his house, and soon joined their society. The magistrates informed Stuyvesant that John Brown's house had become a conventicle for Quakers. Being arrested, he did not deny the charge, and was fined twenty-five pounds and threatened with banishment.

The next week a new proclamation was issued, saying, " The public exercise of any religion but the Reformed, in houses, barns, ships, woods or fields, will be punished by a fine of fifty guilders ; double for the second offence ; and for the third quadruple with arbitrary correction."

John Brown, either unable or refusing to pay his

fine, was taken to New Amsterdam, where he was imprisoned for three months. An order was then issued announcing his banishment.

"For the welfare," it was written, "of the community, and to crush as far as possible, that abominable sect who treat with contempt both the political magistrate, and the ministers of God's holy word, and who endeavor to undermine the police and religion, John Brown is to be transported from this province in the first ship ready to sail, as an example to others."

He was sent to Holland in the "Gilded Fox." Stuyvesant wrote to the Company, "The contumacious prisoner has been banished as a terror to others who, if not discouraged by this example, will be dealt with still more severely."

The Company in Holland, was not at all in sympathy with its intolerant governor. The exile was received by them respectfully. The following dispatch, condemnatory of the severe measures of Stuyvesant, was forwarded to him :

"Although it is our cordial desire that similar and other sectarians may not be found there, yet, as the contrary seems to be the fact, we doubt very much whether vigorous proceedings against them ought not to be discontinued ; unless indeed, you intend to check and destroy your population, which, in the youth of your existence, ought rather to be encouraged by all possible means.

"Wherefore it is our opinion that some connivance is useful, and that at least the consciences of men, ought to remain free and unshackled. Let every one remain free so long as he is modest, irreproachable in his political conduct, and so long as he does not offend others or oppose the government. This maxim of moderation has always been the guide of our magistrates in this city. The consequence has been that people have flocked from every land to this asylum. Tread thus in their steps and we doubt not you will be blessed."

From this time persecution ceased in New Netherland. Either Governor Stuyvesant was convinced by the argument in the above dispatch, or he was intimidated by his rebuke. After two years of absence John Brown returned to New Netherland, and it is said that the governor received him as though he were ashamed of what he had done.

The year 1663 was a year of many disasters. Early in the year an earthquake shook severely the whole of New Netherland and of the adjacent regions. The melting of the snow in the spring, and the falling rains caused a desolating freshet, which inundated all the meadow lands of the rivers, utterly destroying the crops. This calamity was followed by the small-pox, which spread with a like rapidity and fatality among the Europeans and the Indians. Of the Iroquois Indians over a thousand died. In addition to these calamities came, worst of all, war with its indescribable horrors.

At Esopus the hand of industry had been very successfully employed. Quite a crowded population filled the houses, within the palisades, and the rapidly increasing numbers had rendered it necessary to commence another village, which was called Wildwyck, on a fertile plain at a little distance from the fort. Under the blessings of peace, wealth had increased. The church numbered sixty members. Most of the garrison had been withdrawn as no longer needed.

But the Indians could not forget their brethren sent to life-long slavery at Curaçoa. It was increasingly evident that the peace, into which they had entered, was not cordial. It was a compulsory peace. An unendurable outrage had driven them into the war. And by the terms of peace, while they had been compelled to return all the captives they held, fifteen of their warriors were doomed to perpetual slavery.

Murmurings were heard which foreboded an outbreak. Some of the settlers became alarmed and communicated their fears to Governor Stuyvesant.

He sent word that he would soon visit Esopus, to investigate the state of affairs. The Indian chiefs, hearing of this, returned the message, that if he were coming to renew their treaty of friendship they should expect him to come unarmed and they would be happy to meet him in council, according to their custom, in the open field outside of the gate.

It was a pleasant morning of the 7th of June. The governor had not yet arrived. The settlers, thrown off their guard by the friendly message which the chiefs had returned, were scattered about in the fields engaged in their daily avocations. Between eleven and twelve o'clock at noon, an unusual number of savages spread themselves through the villages and entered the dwellings. They were apparently, as usual, entirely unarmed, though it afterwards appeared that they had concealed weapons. They brought corn, beans, and other trifling articles for sale.

Suddenly the war-whoop was uttered from one savage throat as a signal, and was instantly re-echoed by a hundred others. Tomahawks and knives and battle-axes gleamed in the air, and the work of extermination was instantly and energetically commenced. The settlers were taken entirely by surprise. Every Indian had marked his man. Neither women nor children were spared. Those who could not easily be captured were struck down. Many of the Indians speedily regained their guns which they had concealed in the grass. Houses were plundered and set on fire.

But the colonists did not submit to their fate without valiant resistance. For several hours the most deadly battle raged. The yells of the savages, and the shrieks of wounded women and children, devoured by the flames which consumed their dwellings, were awful beyond any power of the pen to describe.

Roelof Swartwout was entrusted with the municipal government at Esopus. His office of Schout somewhat resembled that of a mayor in one of our modern cities. He displayed much presence of mind and bravery on this occasion. Rallying a few bold men around him, he at length succeeded in driving the savages from within the palisades and in shutting the gates. Several hours of this awful conflict had now passed. Evening had come. Devastation, ruin, death surrounded them. The outer village was in ashes. The fields were strewn with the bodies of the dead. The half-burned corpses of women and children were to be seen amidst the smoking cinders of their former homes.

The village within the palisades had been set on

fire. A few houses had been burned, consuming the mangled remains of those who had fallen beneath the tomahawk and battle-axe of the Indian. Fortunately a change of the wind had saved most of the village from destruction. Swartwout and his brave little band, protected by the palisades, were able through the loop-holes, to strike down any Indian, who should appear within reach of their bullets. They were now safe.

But this awful storm of war, which had passed over their beautiful valley had, in three short hours of a summer's afternoon, converted the whole scene into a spectacle of almost unearthly misery. Every dwelling outside of the palisades was in ashes. Several within the enclosure were consumed, and the charred bodies of the dead were intermingled with the blackened timbers. Twenty-one of the settlers had been killed outright. Nine were severely wounded. Forty-five, mostly women and children, were taken captive, to be carried into bondage more dreadful than death.

A night of woe ensued, during which the yells of the savages, in their triumphal orgies dancing around their captives, and probably exposing some to the torture, fell appallingly upon the ears of the sleepless survivors within the gates. Was this God's allowed retribution for the crime of sending the

Indians into slavery? It certainly was the consequence.

The intelligence of this dreadful calamity was immediately transmitted to Governor Stuyvesant at New Amsterdam. Through all the settlements the tidings spread, creating universal panic. Mothers and maidens turned pale as they thought of another Indian war. The farmers and their families, abandoning everything, fled from all directions to the forts within their reach. Every able-bodied man was put to work in strengthening the defences.

The governor promptly dispatched forty-two well-armed men to Esopus. Large bounties were offered to all who would enlist. Forty-six friendly Indians from Long Island offered their services and were accepted as auxiliaries. Ample supplies were forwarded to the devastated village. Scouting parties were sent up the river to search out the savages in their hiding-places. The Mohawks interposed their friendly mediation in behalf of peace, and succeeded in recovering and restoring to the Dutch several captives.

They also informed the governor that the Indians had taken the remaining captives to one of their villages about thirty miles southwest of Esopus, and that they refused to release them unless the governor would send them rich presents and make a

peace without any compensation for what had transpired at Esopus. It seems that the Indians regarded
the massacre there simply as the just atonement
which they had exacted for the enslavement of their
brethren, and that now their rude sense of justice
being satisfied, they were ready to enter into a solid
peace. But the governor was not at all disposed to
regard the matter in this light. He deemed it
necessary, under the circumstances, that the Indians
should feel the full weight of the white man's avenging hand.

Just then a woman, Mrs. Van Imbrock, who had
succeeded in effecting her escape from the Indians,
reached Esopus, having traversed the wilderness
through a thousand perils. She was a woman of
great energy, intelligent and observing, and her
heart was bleeding in view of the friends she had left
behind her in captivity. She was eager to act as a
guide to lead a war-party for the rescue of her
friends in the retreat of the savages. She estimated
their number at about two hundred warriors. They
occupied a square fort, very strongly built of timber.
And still they adopted the precaution of sending
the prisoners every night under strong guard, to
some distant place in the mountains. The Indians
had a very clear appreciation of the value of their
captives as hostages.

Governor Stuyvesant sent a force of two hundred and ten men, under Captain Crygier, to attack them. Forty-one of these were Indians and seven were negroes. They took with them two small cannon, with which at a safe distance, they could soon open a breach through the Indian ramparts, which were merely bullet-proof. A garrison of about seventy men was left behind for the protection of Esopus.

At four o'clock in the afternoon of the 26th of July, this little band commenced its march through the trails of the wilderness, towards the setting sun. The path was a rugged one over high hills and across mountain streams. They had traversed but a few miles when night came on and they bivouacked until daybreak. The next morning they pressed forward with all vigor until they were within about six miles of the fort. One hundred and sixteen men were then sent forward to attack the Indians by surprise, while the remainder prudently followed close after as a reserve.

But the wary Indians, through their scouts, had ascertained the approach of the foe and had fled with their prisoners to the mountains. The Dutch were astonished at the strength of the fort and at the scientific skill with which it was constructed. The Indians had evidently learned not a little of military art from the Europeans. Three parallel rows of palisades enclosed a large square, with loopholes through which unobstructed aim could be taken at assailants. Within the palisades there were strong block-houses, provided also with loopholes, to which houses the warriors could retreat, as to citadels, in case the outer works were taken. Between the houses and the outworks there was a creek. The whole fortress would have been no disgrace to an European engineer.

The party found very comfortable quarters in the fort for the night, and an ample supply of provisions. An Indian woman, not being aware that the white men were in the fort, came back for some article she had left behind. She was taken prisoner and informed her captors of the direction in which the Indians had fled. As it is necessary for such a party of two or three hundred, to keep together, and as the trail through meadows, across streamlets and over mountains is narrow, it is not difficult having once found their track to follow it.

It was determined, after a brief consultation, to pursue them. The next morning at daybreak, the pursuit was commenced. Twenty-five men were left to keep possession of the fort. After several hours of very fatiguing travel, they reached the spot, on a high mountain, where the squaw supposed that the

Indians had established their camp. But not an Indian was there. They had probably left their spies on the path, who had informed them that the foe was at hand.

The woman now said that they must have gone on to another stronghold they had, at the distance of about six miles. The march was continued through great difficulties. But it was fruitless. Not an Indian was to be found. They had another stronghold about twelve miles farther on. It was possible that they might be found there. But all were fatigued and discouraged, and were disposed to give up the hopeless chase. At one time they caught sight of nine savages in the distance, but they fled like deer.

Captain Crygier, deeming all further attempt to overtake the savages hopeless, decided to return to the Indian fort. Having reached it, all hands engaged in the work of destruction. The savages had collected there a large supply of provisions for the approaching winter. The colonists took all they could carry away with them and destroyed the rest. They then utterly demolished the buildings and palisades, committing all to the flames. The works must have cost the Indians an immensity of labor. There were two hundred acres of corn, waving richly in the summer breeze, giving promise of an abund-

11*

ant harvest. All was trampled down. It was a fearful calamity to the wretched Indians. Probably not a few perished of famine the next winter. There was by no means a sufficient supply of game in the forest to meet their wants. Their main reliance was upon their cornfields.

While they were engaged in this work of destruction four savages appeared upon a hill near some of the colonists, and cried out to them "To-morrow we will come and fight you, for we must all now die of hunger."

The next morning the colonists commenced their return. They showed their respect for the prowess of the savages, by forming their little army in strong military array, with the advance, the centre and the rear guard. At nine o'clock in the evening of August 1st, 1663, they reached their anxious friends at Esopus, without the loss of a man.

Ere long news reached Esopus, that the savages were building another fort, which they called a castle, about thirty-six miles southwest of Esopus, probably near the present town of Mamakating, Sullivan county. An expedition of one hundred and twenty five men, under Captain Crygier, was immediately organized to destroy the works. A young Indian guided the party. Several horses were taken with them to bring back those who might be wounded.

At one o'clock in the afternoon of September third, the party set out from Esopus. A march of nine miles brought them to a creek, which was so swollen by recent rains, that they were delayed for several hours until they could construct a rude bridge across it. In the meantime the rain was falling in torrents. It was not until four o'clock in the afternoon of the next day that the party effected its passage across the stream. They then pressed forward twelve miles farther and bivouacked for the night.

At daybreak they were again upon the move, and about two o'clock in the afternoon emerged from the forest in view of the fort. It stood upon an elevated plain. Like the one we have already described, it consisted of a square enclosure, surrounded by two rows of strong palisades, and a third had already been commenced. These posts, pointed at the top, were firmly planted in the ground, and were of the thickness of a man's body, and rose fifteen feet into the air.

Captain Crygier, after carefully scrutinizing the works, divided his force into two sections for the attack. He was well aware that he had a foe to encounter who would fight with the utmost desperation behind his intrenchments. One party of the assailants crept cautiously along, beneath the covert of a hill, until, coming to the open plain, they were discovered by a squaw, who uttered a terrible cry which roused the whole garrison of Indians.

A sudden onslaught was then made by both parties pouring, like an inundation, through the unfinished works into the fort. The savages, taken by surprise, and many of them without their arms, were thrown into a panic. Many of them rushed out of the fort, leaving their guns in the houses behind. The Dutch followed close upon their heels, shooting them, and with keen sabres cutting them down. Just beyond the fort there was a creek. The terrified Indians precipitated themselves into it, and by wading and swimming forced their way across. Here they attempted to rally and opened fire upon the pursuing Dutch. The fire was returned with so much vigor that the Indians were driven with loss from their position. The assailants soon crossed the creek, and the discomfited Indians, in hopeless rout, fled wildly into the trackless wilderness.

In the impetuous assault the chief of the tribe, Papoquanchen, was slain, and fourteen of his warriors with four Indian women and three children Twenty-two christian prisoners were recovered, and fourteen Indians were taken captive. The Dutch lost but three killed and six were wounded. The houses were all plundered by the victors. There was found in them eighty guns, and "bearskins, deerskins, blankets, elk hides and peltries sufficient to load a shallop." Forty rolls of wampum and twenty pounds of powder were also taken. The colonists loaded themselves with such plunder as they could carry. The rest was destroyed.

The return of the victors with the rescued christian captives, gave great joy at Esopus. We regret to record that, on the march home, there was one of the Indian prisoners, an old man, who refused to go any farther. Captain Crygier had him led a few steps out of the path and shot. In unfeeling terms the captain writes, "We carried him a little aside and then gave him his last meal."

The remainder of the month of September was employed in sending out small scouting parties, and in protecting the farmers while gathering their harvests. Though the Esopus Indians were pretty thoroughly crushed by these disasters which had befallen them, they showed no sign of submission. It was estimated that not more than twenty-eight warriors, with fourteen women and a few children survived. And these were without homes and almost in a state of starvation. Still it was decided to fit out a third expedition against them to effect their utter overthrow.

It was thought most probable that the dispersed

Indians would rally again within the fort at Mamakating, which had been captured and sacked but not as yet destroyed. It was perhaps left as a lure to draw the Indians to that point where they could be surrounded and annihilated.

A strong well-armed party of one hundred and sixty-four soldiers set out on this expedition. Forty six of these were friendly Indians from a tribe called Marespincks, whose home was on Long Island. The soldiers were familiar with the route which they had so recently traversed. A weary but rapid march of twenty hours brought them to the scene of their recent victory. Not an Indian was there. All was silence and awful desolation. Even the colonists were appalled by the spectacle which opened before them. The Indians were so thoroughly panic stricken that they had not ventured back even to bury their dead. The decaying corpses lay scattered around, many of them half consumed by vultures and wolves. The birds and beasts, with wild cries, were devouring their prey. Parties were sent out to scour the woods. But no signs of the savages could be found. In fact the Esopus tribe was no more. It was afterwards ascertained that the wretched remnant had fled south and were finally blended and lost among the Minnisincks and other southern tribes.

The fort was so strong that it required not a little labor to destroy it. It was necessary to cut down or dig up the palisades, which were composed of trunks of trees twenty feet long and eighteen inches in diameter. Several cornfields were found in the vicinity wherever an opening in the forest and fertile soil invited the labor of the indolent Indian. Two days were occupied in cutting down the corn, already beautiful in its golden ripeness, and in casting the treasure into the creek. The palisades were then piled around the dwellings and in a few hours nothing remained of the once imposing fortress but smoking embers.

This Indian fort or castle, it is said, stood on the banks of what is now called the Shawangunk kill, in the town of the same name, at the southwestern extremity of Ulster county. It seems as though it were the doom of armies on the march, ever to encounter floods of rain. Scarcely had the troops commenced their return ere the windows of heaven seemed to be opened and the fountains of the great deep to be broken up.

At ten o'clock on the morning of the 5th of October, 1664, the march was commenced. The rain came on like that of Noah's deluge. The short afternoon passed away as, threading ravines and climbing mountains, they breasted the flood and the gale. The drenched host was soon enveloped in the gloom of a long, dark, stormy night. Weary and shelterless, the only couch they could find was the dripping sod, the only canopy, the weeping skies. The weeping skies! yes, nature seemed to weep and mourn over the crimes of a lost race,—over man's inhumanity to man. It was not until the evening of the next day, the rain still continuing, that these weary soldiers reached their home at Esopus.

CHAPTER XII.

Encroachments of the English.

Annihilation of the Esopus Tribe.—The Boundary Question.—Troubles on Long Island. The Dutch and English Villages.—Petition of the English.—Embarrassments of Governor Stuyvesant.—Embassage to Hartford.—The Repulse.—Peril of New Netherland.—Memorial to the Fatherland.—New Outbreak on Long Island.—John Scott and his High-handed Measures.—Strengthening the Fortifications.

ALL but three of the captives carried away by the Esopus Indians, were eventually recovered. The fate of those three is lost in hopeless obscurity. The revelations of the day of Judgment can alone make known their tragic doom. To them, as to thousands of others, this earthly life, if this be all, must have been an unmitigated calamity. But this is not all. After death cometh the judgment. It will be easy for God, in the future world, to compensate his children a thousand-fold for all the ills they are called to suffer in this life. There is true christian philosophy in the beautiful poetry of Bryant,

" Oh, deem not they are blest alone
Whose lives an even tenor keep.
For God, who pities man, hath shown
A blessing for the eyes that weep.

"For God has marked each sorrowing day
And numbered every secret tear,
And heaven's long age of bliss shall pay
For all his children suffer here."

Peace was now restored by the annihilation of the hostile Indians. Most of the Dutch soldiers returned to New Amsterdam. Still it was deemed important to enlarge and strengthen the fortifications at Esopus.

The boundary line between the British colonies in New England, and the Dutch settlements in New Netherland, still continued in dispute. The English, in numerical strength, were in the vast ascendency, and could easily overpower the Dutch. Very strenuous efforts had been made, by the States-General, to lead the British government to accept some boundary line. But all was in vain. It was very evident that the English intended to claim the whole. And it was also evident that their colonies were increasing so rapidly that, in a short time, they would be able to take possession of all the territory so strongly that it would be hopeless for the Dutch to attempt any resistance.

Governor Stuyvesant now received intelligence from Holland that there was no hope of any settlement being effected through the two governments, and that he must do everything in his power to strengthen the boundary lines the Dutch claimed, and to enter into such friendly relations with the New England colonists that they should not be tempted to undertake any encroachments. To add to the governor's embarrassments very many English-men had taken up their residence in the Dutch set-tlements, particularly on Long Island. Though they had, of necessity, taken the oath of allegiance to the constituted authorities, their sympathies were with the New England colonists; and they would wel-come any revolution which should transfer the terri-tory to Great Britain, and thus absolve them from their oaths.

In accordance with the instructions received from Holland, the governor repaired to Boston to enter into a friendly conference with the authorities there. Scarcely had he left New Amsterdam, when an English emissary, James Christie, visited Graves-end, Flushing, Hempstead and Jamaica, with the announcement that the inhabitants of those places were no longer under the Dutch government, but that their territory was annexed to the Connecticut colony. This important movement took place on the sixth of September, 1663.

Only about six weeks before, the Connecticut council, on the 20th of July, had sent Captain John Talcott with an armed force of eighteen soldiers, to

that portion of New Netherland now called Westchester, to declare that the inhabitants were absolved from their allegiance to the Dutch government,
to dismiss the old magistrates and to appoint others
in their stead. These were high-handed measures, apparently inexcusable.

When John Christie reached Gravesend, he summoned the whole village together and read to them
the dispatch. The British element was there
strongly in the ascendency, even the magistrates
being mainly on that side. As Christie was reading
the treasonable document, one of the Dutch magistrates, sheriff Stillwell, faithful to his oath, arrested
him. The other magistrates ordered the arrest of
Stillwell. His life was in danger from the passions of
the mob. He succeeded in sending word to New
Amsterdam of the peril of his condition. A sergeant
and eight soldiers were dispatched, who arrested
Christie again and held him under their guard.

News of these agitations spread rapidly through
the adjoining villages. It was rumored that a large
mob was gathering to rescue Christie from the
soldiers. Consequently, two hours after midnight,
under protection of darkness and without the
knowledge of the community, Christie was secretly
removed from sheriff Stillwell's house to New Amsterdam. During the next day the tidings of his

removal spread through the streets. It created great exasperation. At night a mob of one hundred and fifty men surrounded the house of sheriff Stillwell, shouting that they would have him, dead or alive.

He succeeded in the darkness, in escaping by the back door, and in finding his way to the house of his son-in-law. The mob broke in, ransacked his house in every corner, poured down their own thirsty throats a large quantity of brandy which they found there, and dispersed without committing any further depredations.

Stillwell hastened to New Amsterdam, to enter his complaints there, and to seek protection. The other magistrates wrote, throwing all the blame upon him, accusing him of having acted in a violent manner and of causing "a great hubbub in the town." " We are," they wrote, " the loyal subjects of the Dutch government, but not of sheriff Stillwell, who is the greatest disturber of the peace who ever came among us."

The excitement was great. Threats were uttered of retaliation if Christie were not released. But the Dutch council in New Amsterdam approved of the conduct of its sheriff. Christie was held firmly. Dispatches were sent to all the towns in western Long Island, where there was a considerable English

population, ordering that any seditious persons who
should visit their settlements, should be arrested
and sent to New Amsterdam. They then sent an
express to Governor Stuyvesant in Boston, that he
might bring the question of these disorderly measures before the General Assembly there.

But the governor could obtain no redress and no
promises of amendment. The Massachusetts authorities would not hold themselves bound to the
faithful observance of the treaty of 1650. They
said that it was subject to his Majesty's approval
and to any limitations which might be found in the
charter granted to Connecticut. They refused to
submit the question to any arbitrators whatever.
The New England colonists were conscious that the
power was in their own hands, and they were disposed to use it.

In the meantime the English residents in the
settlements on western Long Island were not idle.
The following very emphatic petition was got up
and signed by twenty-six individuals:

"The humble petition of us the inhabitants of
Jamaica, Middleborough and Hempstead, Long Isl-
and, whose names are subscribed, to the honored
General Court, to be assembled at Hartford on the
8th of October, 1663, humbly showeth,

"That forasmuch as it has pleased the all-dispos-

ing Providence to appoint unto us our dwellings in
these parts of the country, under the Dutch government, in which government we meet with several
inconveniences, which do much to trouble us, and
which we find very uncomfortable, and forasmuch
as we have received information how it hath pleased the Highest Majesty to move the heart of the
King's Majesty to grant unto your colony such enlargements as comprehend the whole island, thereby opening a way for us, as we hope, from our present bondage, to such liberties and enlargements as
your patent affords,

" Our humble petition is that, as we are already,
according to our best information, under the skirts of
your patent, so you would be pleased to cast over us
the skirts of your government and protection ; for as-
suredly if you should leave us now, which we hope we
have not cause to fear, our lives, comforts and estates
will be much endangered, as woful experience makes
manifest. For a countryman of ours, for carrying a
message to a neighbor plantation, from some of yourselves, has been imprisoned for several weeks, and
how long it will be continued we know not."

This last sentence had reference to John Christie. It must be admitted that this was a very mild
way of putting the question, when it is remembered
that he came, commissioned by the Connecticut au-

thorities, at least so he represented it, to announce to the people in the Dutch settlements, that they were no longer under the Dutch government, but under that of Hartford.

This petition was speedily followed by vigorous measures, which were undoubtedly countenanced, if not authorized, by the Connecticut authorities. One Richard Panton, "whose commission was his sword and whose power his pistol," threatened the people of Flatbush and other Dutch villages in the neighborhood, with the pillage of their property unless they would take the oath of allegiance to the Hartford government and take up arms against the Dutch provincial authorities.

Such were the news which first greeted Governor Stuyvesant when he returned, not a little dispirited, from his unsuccessful mission to Boston. He was fully aware that he could bring forward no physical power which could resist the encroachments of his unscrupulous neighbors. He had no weapon to which he could resort but diplomatic skill. He accordingly immediately sent a deputation of four of his principal men to Hartford, still to make another attempt with the authorities there to settle the boundary question, "so that all further disputes may, for the welfare of our mutual subjects, be prevented."

The commissioners sailed from New Amsterdam and after two days landed at Milford. Thence they took horses and rode to New Haven, where they passed the night. The next day they rode to Hartford. The road through the almost unbroken wilderness was rough and the journey very fatiguing. It took our fathers four days to traverse the space over which we can now easily pass in four hours. The General Assembly at Hartford appointed three persons as a committee of conference to meet the delegation from New Amsterdam. A long negotiation followed. John Winthrop, son of Governor Winthrop of Massachusetts, was then governor of Connecticut. He seems to have been the worthy son of his noble sire. His sense of justice disposed him to respect the claims of the Dutch delegation. He admitted that the patent issued by the king of England could by no justice rob the Dutch of their territory, and that it was not so intended. But the Hartford commissioners were inexorable. "The opinion of the governor," they said, "is but the opinion of one man. The grant of the king of England includes all the land south of the Boston line to Virginia and to the Pacific Ocean. We do not know any New Netherland, unless you can show a patent for it from the king of England:"

"But did you not," said the Dutch delegates,

12

"agree by the treaty of 1650, that the boundary
line on Long Island should run from the western
part of Oyster bay straight across the island to the
sea; and that the land east of that line should belong
to the English and west to the Dutch?

"And did you not agree that, on the mainland,
the boundary line between the Dutch and English
possessions should begin upon the west side of
Greenwich bay, running twenty miles into the unknown interior, and that the region west of that
should belong to the Dutch?"

The emphatic reply to those questions was, "We
regard that treaty as an absolute nullity—of no force.
We shall govern ourselves entirely by the patent
granted us by his majesty the king of England.
The Dutch may hold as much as they now actually
occupy. But that shall not hinder us from taking
possession of any territory not occupied by them."

The Dutch then proposed, by way of compromise,
that for the present, Westchester should remain in
possession of Connecticut, while the towns on western Long Island should remain under the government of New Netherland. To this the Hartford
commissioners replied:

"We do not know of any province of New
Netherland. There is a Dutch governor over a
Dutch plantation on the island of Manhattan. Long

Island is included in our patent, and we shall possess and maintain it." *

Thus repulsed at every point, the Dutch agents commenced their return. They bore a letter to Stuyvesant from the General Assembly, in which, withholding from him the title of governor of New Netherland, they discourteously addressed him simply as " Director General at Manhattan."

As we have mentioned, there were many English settlers in the Dutch towns on the western end of Long Island. In some of them it is not improbable that the English element predominated. In the letter sent by the General Court to Governor Stuyvesant, it was stated that Westchester and Stamford belonged to Connecticut; that, for the present, the General Court would forbear from exercising any authority over the English plantations on Long Island; but that, should the Dutch molest the English there, the Connecticut authorities would use all just and lawful means for their protection.

The situation of the Dutch province was now alarming in the extreme, and Governor Stuyvesant was environed by difficulties which no mortal sagacity or energy could surmount. His treasury was exhausted. The English settlers in the Long Island

* See Brodhead's State of New York, vol. 1. p. 721 ; also O'Callaghan's New Netherland, vol 2. p. 489.

villages, were in determined and open revolt. And his English neighbors, whom he was altogether too feeble to resist, were crowding upon him in the most merciless encroachments.

Under these circumstances, he called a Convention, to consist of two delegates from all the neighboring villages, to meet at New Amsterdam on the 22d of October, 1663. Eight towns were represented.

The Convention adopted an earnest remonstrance to the authorities in Holland, in which the disastrous situation of the province was mainly attributed to their withholding that aid which was essential to the maintenance of the colony.

"The people of Connecticut," the remonstrance stated, "are enforcing their unlimited patent according to their own interpretation, and the total loss of New Netherland is threatened. The English, to cloak their plans, now object that there is no proof, no legal commission or patent, from their High Mightinesses, to substantiate and justify our rights and claims to the property of this province, and insinuate that through the backwardness of their High Mightinesses to grant such a patent, you apparently intended to place the people here on slippery ice, giving them lands to which your honors had no right whatever."

Governor Stuyvesant sent with this remonstrance a private letter to the home government, in which he urged that the boundary question should be settled by the national authorities of the two countries. "It is important," he said, "that the States-General should send letters to the English villages on Long Island, commanding them to return to their allegiance. And that the objections of Connecticut may be met, the original charter of the West India Company should be solemnly confirmed by a public act of their High Mightinesses, under their great seal, which an Englishman commonly dotes upon like an idol."

Scarcely were these documents dispatched when new and still more alarming outbreaks occurred. Two Englishmen, Anthony Waters of Hempstead, and John Coe of Middlebury, with an armed force of nearly one hundred men, visited most of what were called the English villages, convoked the people, told them that their country belonged to the king of England, and that they must no longer pay taxes to the Dutch. They removed the magistrates and appointed their own partisans in their stead. They then visited the Dutch towns and threatened them with the severest vengeance if they did not renounce all allegiance to the Dutch authorities, and take the oath of fealty to the king of England.

Only four weeks after this, another party of
twenty Englishmen from Gravesend, Flushing and
Jamaica, secretly entered Raritan river, in a sloop,
and sailing up the river several miles, assembled the
chiefs of some of the neighboring tribes, and endeavored to purchase of them a large extent of territory
in that region.   They knew perfectly well not only
that they were within the bounds which had been
the undisputed possession of New Netherland for
nearly half a century, but that the Dutch had also
purchased of the Indians all their title to these lands.

Stuyvesant, being informed of this procedure,
promptly sent Ensign Crygier, with an armed force,
in a swift sailing yacht, to find the English and
thwart their measures.   At the same time he sent
Hans, a friendly Indian, in whom he could repose
confidence, to warn the sachems against selling
over again, lands to which they no longer had any
title.   The Dutch party reached the spot where the
Englishmen and the Indians were in council, just in
time to stop the sale.   The Indians were shrewd
enough to know that all they could give was a " quit
claim " title, and they were very willing to give that
in view of the rich remuneration which was offered
them.

The English thus baffled, again took their sloop
and sailed down the bay, to a point between Rens-

selaer's Hook and Sandy Hook, where they were about to renew their endeavors when Ensign Crygier again overtook them. "You are traitors," he exclaimed. "You are acting against the government to which you have taken the oath of fidelity." " This whole country," they replied, " has been given to the English by his Majesty the king of England."

Thus the antagonistic parties separated. The Dutch sloop returned to New Amsterdam. The next day a number of sachems came to New Amsterdam and sold to Governor Stuyvesant the remainder of the lands on the Raritan, which had not previously been transferred to the Dutch.

One John Scott, an Englishman of turbulent character, and a zealous royalist, petitioned king Charles Second to bestow upon him the government of Long Island. In his petition, which was referred to the Council for Foreign Plantations, he said :

" The Dutch have of late years, unjustly obtruded upon and possessed themselves of certain places on the mainland of New England, and some islands adjacent, as in particular on Manhattan and Long Island, being the true and undoubted inheritance of his Majesty."

In reply to this petition, Scott with two others,

was appointed a committee to prepare "a statement
of the English title to those lands; with an account
of the Dutch intrusion, their deportment since and
management of that possession, their strength, trade
and government there, and of the means to make
them acknowledge and submit to his Majesty's government or by force to expulse them."

Armed with this authority, Scott came to
America, where he was very cordially received by
the authorities in New Haven.   Connecticut invested him with the powers of a magistrate throughout the whole of Long Island, and Governor John
Winthrop administered to him the oath of office.
Scott entered vigorously upon his work of wresting
western Long Island from the dominion of the
Dutch, whom he denounced as "cruel and rapacious
neighbors who were enslaving the English settlers."

He visited most of the villages, where large
numbers of the English resided, but found that
there was strong opposition to being annexed to
Connecticut.   Many of them, particularly the Bap-
tists and the Quakers, were very unwilling to come
under the rule of the Puritan government.

Consequently, six of the towns, Hempstead,
Gravesend, Flushing, Middlebury, Jamaica and
Oyster Bay, formed a combination to govern them-
selves independently of Connecticut, and empowered

Scott to act as their President, until the king of England should establish a permanent government among them. Scott in his pride now unfurled an almost imperial banner. Placing himself at the head of one hundred and seventy armed men, horse and foot, he set out to compel the neighboring Dutch villages to renounce their allegiance to Holland and to subject themselves to his sway.

He first marched upon Brooklyn. Summoning the citizens, he told them that the soil they occupied belonged to the king of England, and that he now claimed it as his own, and that they were consequently absolved from all further allegiance to the Dutch government and were required to take the oath of submission to the new government, now about to be established over them.

Scott was accompanied by so powerful an armed force that the magistrates could not arrest him. One of them, however, Secretary Van Ruyven, invited him to cross the river to New Amsterdam and confer with the governor there. Scott replied, " Let Stuyvesant come here with a hundred men; I will wait for him and run my sword through his body."

There was no disposition manifested whatever, on the part of the people, to renounce the government of their fathers and accept of that of Scott in

12*

its stead. There was a little boy standing by, whose proud and defiant bearing arrested the attention of Scott. He was a son of the heroic Crygier, of whom we have before spoken. Scott ordered him to take off his hat and bow to the flag of England. The boy refused. Scott struck him. A bystander scornfully said, " If you have blows to give, you should strike men, not boys."

Four of Scott's soldiers fiercely assailed the man, and though for a moment he defended himself with an axe, he was soon compelled to fly. Scott demanded his surrender and threatened to lay the town in ashes unless he were given up. He was not surrendered, and Scott did not venture to execute his barbarous threat.

From Brooklyn Scott went to Flatbush. He there unfurled the flag of England in front of the house of the sheriff. Curiosity assembled a large concourse to witness what was transpiring. Scott addressed them at much length. " He jabbered away," writes a Dutch historian, " in English, like a mountebank."

" This land," said he, " which you now occupy, belongs to his Majesty, king Charles. He is the right and lawful lord of all America, from Virginia to Boston. Under his government you will enjoy more freedom than you ever before possessed.

Hereafter you shall pay no more taxes to the Dutch government, neither shall you obey Peter Stuyvesant. He is no longer your governor, and you are not to acknowledge his authority. If you refuse to submit to the king of England, you know what to expect."

His harangue produced no effect. The Dutch remained unshaken in their loyalty. Some of the magistrates ventured to tell him that these were matters which he ought to settle with Governor Stuyvesant. He replied,

" Stuyvesant is governor no longer. I will soon go to New Amsterdam, with a hundred men, and proclaim the supremacy of his Majesty, king Charles, beneath the very walls of the fort."

The next day he went to Flatbush, where there was a renewal of the scenes which we have above described. Though the people could present no resistance, he found no voice to cheer him. The want of success exasperated Scott. He went to New Utrecht. There was a block fort there, armed with cannon, and over which floated the Dutch flag. He hauled down that banner and raised in its stead the flag of England. Then, with Dutch cannon and Dutch powder, he fired a salute in honor of his victory. All passers-by were ordered to uncover their heads and bow in submission to the

English flag. Those who refused to do so were pursued by his soldiers and cruelly beaten.

Governor Stuyvesant, upon being informed of these transactions, immediately sent three of his principal men to Long Island, to seek some arrangement with Scott for the termination of such disorders. They met him at Jamaica. After much discussion they entered into a partial agreement, which, was to be submitted to the approval of Governor Stuyvesant. As the Dutch deputies took their leave, Scott said to them,

"This whole island belongs to the king of England. He has made a grant of it to his brother, the duke of York. He knows that it will yield him an annual revenue of one hundred and fifty thousand dollars. He is soon coming with an ample force, to take possession of his property. If it is not surrendered peaceably he is determined to take, not only the whole island, but also the whole province of New Netherland."

With these alarming tidings, the Dutch envoys returned to New Amsterdam. Disorders were now rapidly multiplying. Scott rallied around him all the most turbulent of the English population, and the Dutch towns were menaced with violence. The Dutch families in the English villages, were many of them compelled to abandon their houses, and re pair to the Dutch villages for protection. Frequent collisions occurred. There was no longer any happiness or peace to be found in these dwellings agitated by the approaching tempests of revolution.

The inhabitants of New Amsterdam became greatly alarmed from fear that their rich and beautiful city would be attacked or plundered by the English. The burgomasters and principal men drew up a petition to the authorities urging additional fortifications for the city and the enlistment of an increased armed force."

In this petition they said, " this capital is adorned with so many noble buildings, at the expense of so many good and faithful inhabitants, principally Netherlanders, that it nearly excels any other place in North America. Were it duly fortified it would instil fear into any envious neighbors. It would protect both the East and the North rivers, the surrounding villages and farms, as well as full ten thousand inhabitants who would soon flock to this province, where thousands of acres of land remain wild and uncultivated. It would become the granary of fatherland. Yes, if permitted to abide in peace this land will become an emporium to fatherland by its growing plantations."

In accordance with this memorial, heavy taxes were imposed and large contributions subscribed to enlarge and strengthen the fortifications. A militia of two hundred men was organized, and one hundred and sixty were enlisted as regular soldiers.

CHAPTER XIII.

Hostile Measures Commenced.

John Scott and his Movements.—Losses of the Dutch.—The First General Assembly.—Action of the Home Government.—Peace with the Indians.—Arrest of John Scott.—Governor Winthrop's visit to Long Island.—Sailing of the Fleet.—Preparations for War.—The False Dispatches.—Arrival of the Fleet.—The Summons to Surrender.

GOVERNOR STUYVESANT, with much anxiety of mind, kept a vigilant eye upon the proceedings of John Scott, on Long Island. Some praised the governor for the forbearance he had exhibited under the provoking circumstances. Others severely blamed him for his course, which they pronounced to be cowardly and disgraceful to the nation.

By the terms of the Convention, concluded between the Dutch delegates and John Scott, it was agreed that the English villages, on the western part of Long Island, should remain unmolested under English rule, for the space of one year, until the king of England and the States-General of Holland should have time to settle the question in dispute. In the meantime the English were to have free access to all the Dutch towns on the island, and on the mainland, for purposes of trade; and the Dutch were to enjoy the same privilege in visiting the English towns.

These terms were to be presented to Governor Stuyvesant for his rejection or approval. Deciding to ratify them he took with him an escort of ten men, and proceeded to Hempstead, on the third day of March, 1664. Here he met the President, John Scott, with delegates from the English towns, and the agreement was ratified.

The Dutch had now lost, one after another, every portion of territory which the English had assailed. The whole valley of the Connecticut river had been surrendered to the English. Westchester was entirely in their possession. And now the important towns of Flushing, Jamaica, Hempstead and Gravesend were yielded up to them. The whole of Long Island was also peremptorily claimed by the English, with the declaration that if any resistance were made to their taking possession of it, they would seize the valley of the Hudson and the whole of New Netherland.

The conjuncture was gloomy indeed. Governor Stuyvesant was conscious that he was utterly powerless. He then decided it to be necessary to call to his aid popular representation. A General Assembly of delegates from all the towns was convoked to take into consideration the state of the province. This important meeting was held in the City Hall of New Amsterdam, on the 10th of April, 1664. Twenty-four delegates were present from twelve towns.

Immediately there arose an unfriendly controversy between the governor and the assembly which was fatal to any harmonious or efficient action. The assembly refused to grant the governor the supplies, in money or in men, which he called for, and adjourned for a week. In the meantime Governor Stuyvesant had received dispatches from Holland. The West India Company had acted energetically upon the subject urged in his memorial. They had presented to the States-General a very earnest petition.

In this memorial they laid before that august body, a detailed account of the aggressions committed by the English, and of the repulse with which the Dutch overtures for an amicable settlement had been met at Boston and Hartford.

" Out of respect," said they, " to the alliance recently entered into with England, they had hitherto abstained from hostilities. But, as it now seemed absolutely necessary to repel aggression by force, they implored such military and pecuniary aid as the occasion required.   They also urged that, in conformity with Governor Stuyvesant's request, an act should be passed under the great seal, confirming their original charter; and that letters might be sent to the revolted towns on Long Island, requiring them, under the severest penalties, to return to their allegiance.   In conclusion they asked that the whole of the aggressions of which they complained might be communicated to the king of England, with the request that he would order his English subjects to restore, on the instant, the places they had seized, and to abstain from all further innovations, pending the negotiations for a boundary line."

These requests were complied with by the States-General.   They sent sixty soldiers to New Amsterdam, with orders to Governor Stuyvesant to resist any further encroachments of the English, and to reduce the revolted villages to allegiance.   It was easy for the States-General to issue such an order, but it was not so easy for Governor Stuyvesant to execute it.   The Assembly was immediately called together again, and the documents from Holland presented to them.   After much deliberation it was decided to be impossible, with the force at the governor's command, to subdue the English villages. In those villages it was said that the Dutch were outnumbered six to one; and that upon the outbreak of hostilities, the flourishing settlements on the Connecticut would immediately send such a force to Long Island, as would enable them to overcome and take possession of all the other villages.

It will be remembered that the Esopus Indians had been completely humbled, and almost annihilated. The tribe living in the immediate vicinity of the village of Esopus, had been slaughtered or driven from their lands. The survivors had taken refuge with other neighboring tribes, who were more or less in sympathy with them. Thus while there was a cessation of actual war, hostility continued. No terms of peace had been agreed to, and there could be no friendly intercourse.

News reached Governor Stuyvesant that the Connecticut people, in their intrigues to get possession of New Netherland, were tampering with these river Indians, endeavoring to enter into a treaty of alliance, offensive and defensive with them. It was consequently deemed desirable immediately to secure a general peace with these Indians.

The sachems of several tribes were invited to assemble in the Council Chamber at fort Amsterdam. The governor with nine of his council, met them. It is worthy of special notice that, the preliminaries being settled, one of the Indian chiefs offered an earnest prayer. First he called several times, with a loud voice, upon the Great Spirit to hear him. In his language Bachtamo was the name for God.

"Oh Bachtamo," he said, "help us to make a good treaty with the Dutch. And may the treaty we are about to negotiate be like the stick I hold in my hand. Like this stick may it be firmly united, the one end to the other."

Then turning to the governor, he said, "We all desire peace. I have come with my brother sachems, in behalf of the Esopus Indians, to conclude a peace as firm and compact as my arms, which I now fold together."

Then presenting his hand to Governor Stuyvesant he added, "What I now say is from the fullness of my heart. Such is my desire, and that of all my people."

A solemn treaty was soon negotiated. It was signed the next day, and the event was celebrated by salvos of artillery. On the whole, the terms were fair, but rather hard for the Indians. The treaty is concisely given by O'Callaghan in the following words:

"By its terms all that had passed was to be forever forgotten and forgiven. The land, already given to the Dutch as an indemnity, and now again conquered by the sword, the two forts belonging to the Indians included, became the property of the christians. The savages were not to return thither to plant, nor to visit the village, or any remote Dutch settlements with or without arms. But as it was not intended to expel them altogether from the country, they were permitted to plant near their new fort, and this year only, by their old castle, as they had already placed some seed in the ground there. But the lands, in the neighborhood of these forts, having been conquered, were to belong to the Dutch.

"To prevent all future collision, no savage should hereafter approach the place where the christians were ploughing, pasturing, sowing or engaged in agricultural labor. The violation of this article was to subject them to arrest. They might sell meat or maize at the Ronduit, in parties of three canoes at a time, but only on condition that they sent a flag of truce beforehand to give notice of their approach. For their accommodation, on such occasions, a house was to be built beyond the kill.

"Should a Dutchman kill an Indian, or an Indian a Dutchman, no war was to be declared. A complaint was to be lodged against the murderer, who should be hanged in the presence of both the contracting parties. All damages, by the killing of

cattle, were to be paid for; and this treaty was to
be annually ratified by the Esopus Indians. The
Hackingsack and Staten Island sachems were security for the faithful observance of this contract;
and were bound to co-operate against either the
Esopus Indians or the Dutch, whichever might violate its terms."

The peace thus secured gave universal satisfaction in the Dutch settlements. Governor Stuyvesant devoutly proclaimed a day of general thanksgiving to God for the great blessing.

It will be remembered that John Scott had
received a commission from Connecticut, and it
was expected that, as their agent, he would cause
the English towns on western Long Island to be
annexed to the Connecticut province. Instead
of this, those towns declared themselves independent, and Scott allowed himself to be chosen their
president. The Court at Hartford, upon being
made acquainted with these facts, was very indignant. A proclamation was soon issued by
the Assembly of Connecticut, charging Scott with
various high crimes and misdemeanors, and ordering his arrest. A party of soldiers was sent
under the command of John Allyn, secretary, "to
seize on the body of John Scott." Mr. Allyn
returned to the Honorable Court the follow-

ing interesting report of his procedure on the occasion:

"When we came within sight of the house of John Scott we saw him draw forth those men which came from New Haven to aid him, with some others, unto a body. When we came up towards the house, within twenty or thirty rods thereof, John Scott commanded us, in his Majesty's name to stand, upon our peril. John Scott charged us in his Majesty's name, to get off from his land. John Scott desired to know what our business was.

"Then it was replied, by Nathaniel Seely, that he desired a parley. John Scott granted a parley, and we met, each of us with a couple of musketeers. Then Nathaniel Seely told him that he had come to arrest him, and read the commission unto him. When it was read Seely demanded of him whether he would surrender himself according to commission?

"John Scott replied that he would sacrifice his heart's blood on the ground, before he would yield to him or any of Connecticut jurisdiction. With that the New Haven men answered, 'So will we.' John Scott said, 'Stay awhile and I will fetch you a letter, from under Governor Winthrop's hand, which I do not question much will satisfy you.' So he went into the house and fetched it forth and read it before us, bearing date as he said, of March 25, 1664.

"It was concerning the governor's desiring him to meet him to end some difference in the Narragansett country about a tract of land. John Scott said, 'If you will return to your body, I will fetch a commission under his Majesty's hand, which shall command you all.' Whereupon he made a flourish and said that he would go down unto the face of the company and read it, and he would see if the proudest of them all dared to lay hands upon him. 'Let them,' said he, 'take me if they dare.'

"Then he came down to the head of the company, and read the commission, which he said had the seal manual upon it. Whereupon he renewed his challenge that he would see if the proudest of them all dared to lay hands upon him. Then Nathaniel Seely arrested him in his Majesty's name to go with him according to law."

Scott was taken to Hartford and thrown into jail, where, it is said, he experienced much harsh usage. Soon after this Governor John Winthrop, from Hartford, visited the English Long Island towns, removed the officers appointed by Scott, and installed others who would be devoted to the interests of Connecticut.

Governor Stuyvesant being informed of his presence, immediately crossed the East river to Long Island, to meet the Connecticut governor, who was thus encroaching upon the Dutch domains. He urged upon Governor Winthrop the claims of Holland upon New Netherland, by the apparently indubitable title of discovery, purchase and possession, as well as by the clearly defined obligations of the Hartford treaty of 1650. It will be remembered that by that treaty it was expressly agreed that,

"Upon Long Island a line run from the westernmost part of Oyster Bay, in a straight and direct line to the sea, shall be the bounds between the English and the Dutch there; the easterly part to belong to the English, the westernmost part to the Dutch."

But here was Governor Winthrop, in total disregard of this treaty, many miles west of this line, endeavoring to wrest several towns from the Dutch dominion, and to annex them to the Connecticut colony. All Governor Stuyvesant's arguments were unavailing. Governor Winthrop paid no heed to them. He knew very well that the Dutch governor had no military power with which to enforce his claims. Governor Winthrop therefore contented himself with simply declaring that the whole of Long Island belonged to the king of England.

"All Governor Stuyvesant could adduce," writes

13

O'Callaghan, " was of no avail. The country was the king's, the people his subjects. When priority of title from the Indians was invoked, those from whom the Dutch purchased were, it was replied, not the right owners and had no right to sell. But when deeds which the English held from natives, happened to be older than those of their opponents, then the title could not be gainsayed. All must be received without contradiction.

"The truth is, the Directors in Holland were mistaken in their reliance upon Winthrop's friendship. He now manifested the greatest hostility to the Dutch, and was the head and front of all the opposition they experienced. He was no doubt well-advised of the designs of the Duke of York, and of his brother the king of England, which were about to develop themselves against this province."

While New Netherland was thus fearfully menaced by England, the internal affairs of the province were in a state of prosperity. The rich soil was producing abundant harvests and farms were extending in all directions. Emigrants were continually arriving and were delighted with their new homes. The population of the province now amounted to full ten thousand. New Amsterdam was a flourishing city, containing fifteen hundred inhabitants.

This prosperity excited both the jealousy and

the covetousness of the British court. The king resolved, by one bold blow, to rob Holland of all her American possessions. On the 12th of March, 1664, the king of England granted to his brother James, the Duke of York, the whole of Long Island, all the islands in its neighborhood, and all the lands and rivers from the west side of Connecticut river to the east side of Delaware Bay. This sweeping grant included the whole of New Netherland. This was emphatically expelling the Dutch from the New World.

The first intimation Governor Stuyvesant received of this alarming movement came to him from Boston. A young man, named Ford, brought the tidings to New Amsterdam that a fleet of armed ships had sailed from the naval depot in Portsmouth, England, to enter the Hudson river and take possession of the whole territory. This intelligence created not a little panic. The governor summoned his council, and it was decided to exert every energy in fortifying the city. The hostile fleet might make its appearance any day.

Money was raised. Powder was ordered from the forts on the Delaware. Agents were sent to New Haven to purchase provisions. As it was expected that the fleet would come through the Sound, agents were stationed along the shore, to transmit the tidings of its approach, so soon as the sails should be seen in the distant horizon. Several vessels on the point of sailing with supplies to Curaçoa were detained.

So secretly had the British government moved in this enterprise, that the governmental authorities, in Holland, had not the slightest suspicion of the peril to which their colony in New Netherland was exposed. At the moment when all was agitation in New Amsterdam, and every hand was busy preparing for the defence, Governor Stuyvesant received dispatches from Holland, assuring him that no apprehension of danger from England need be entertained.

"The king of England," it was said, "is only desirous of reducing his colonies to uniformity in Church and State. With this view he has dispatched some commissioners with two or three frigates, to New England, to introduce Episcopacy in that quarter."

It was supposed in Holland, that this intolerant policy would strengthen the Dutch interests in America; that the religious freedom, which the States-General insisted upon, would invite to New Netherland from all the countries of Europe, those who were not willing to conform to the doctrines and ritual of the Church of England.

Governor Stuyvesant, upon receiving these dispatches from the home government, felt relieved of all anxiety. He had no doubt that the previous rumor which had reached him was false. Neither he nor his council anticipated any difficulty. The whole community indulged in the sense of security. The work on the fortifications was stopped; the vessels sailed to Curaçoa, and the governor went up the river to fort Orange. A desolating war had broken out between the Indian tribes there, which raged with such ferocity that the colonists were full of alarm for their own lives and property.

But the English fleet was rapidly approaching. It consisted of four frigates, containing in all an armament of ninety-four guns. This was a force to which defenceless New Amsterdam could present no resistance.

The fleet put into Boston the latter part of July, and the commissioners applied to both Massachusetts and Connecticut for aid in their military expedition against the Dutch. But the Puritans of Massachusetts found innumerable obstacles in the way of rendering any assistance. They feared that the king of England, having reduced the Dutch, would be induced to extend his arbitrary sway, both civil and religious, over those colonists who were

exiles from their native land, simply that they might
enjoy freedom to worship God.

Connecticut, however, hoped that the conquest of
New Netherland might annex the magnificent domain to their own region. Governor Winthrop, of
Hartford, manifested so much alacrity in the cause,
that he was invited to meet the British squadron,
at the west end of Long Island, to which point it
would sail with the first fair wind.

Colonel Richard Nicholls was in command of the
expedition. Three commissioners were associated
with him. They had received instructions to visit
the several New England colonies, and to require
them, "to join and assist vigorously in reducing
the Dutch to subjection." The Duke of York, soon
after the departure of the squadron, conveyed to
Lord Berkeley and Sir George Carteret all the territory between the Hudson and Delaware rivers, from
Cape May north to forty-one degrees and forty
minutes of latitude, "hereafter to be called Nova
Cæsarea or New Jersey."

A friend of Governor Stuyvesant, in Boston, sent
word to New Amsterdam of the arrival of the fleet
and its destination. An express was instantly dispatched to Albany to recall the Governor. He hurried back to the capitol, much chagrined by the
thought that he had lost three weeks. Every able

bodied man was immediately summoned to work at
the city defences, "with spade, shovel and wheelbarrow." This working party was divided into three
classes, one of which was to labor every day. A
permanent guard was organized. The brewers were
forbidden to malt any more grain, that it all might
be reserved for food. Six pieces of cannon were
added to the fourteen already mounted. The garrison at Esopus was summoned to the defence.

About the 20th of August, the English squadron anchored in Nyack Bay, just below the Narrows,
between New Utrecht and Coney Island. A strict
blockade of the river was established. All communication between Long Island and Manhattan was
cut off. Several vessels were captured. Upon
Staten Island, about three miles from where the
frigates rode at anchor, there was a small fort, a
block-house, about twenty feet square. It had
been constructed for defence against the savages.
For its armament it had two small guns, carrying
one pound balls, and a garrison of six old invalid
soldiers. A party was sent on shore, in the boats,
which captured the fort and also a lot of cattle.

The next morning, which was Saturday, Colonel
Nicholls sent a delegation of four men up to fort
Amsterdam, with a summons for the surrender of
"the town situated on the island commonly known

by the name of Manhattoes, with all the forts thereunto belonging." At the same time proclamations
were scattered abroad, forbidding the farmers from
furnishing any supplies to the Dutch garrison, under
penalty of having their houses fired. All the inhabitants of the surrounding villages, who would quietly submit to his Britannic Majesty, were promised
the safe possession of their property. Those who
should otherwise demean themselves were threatened with all the miseries of war.

Governor Stuyvesant had but one hundred soldiers in garrison. He could not place much reliance
upon the aid of undisciplined citizens. Still his
brave spirit was disposed to present a desperate
resistance. He called his council together, but
was unwilling to have the people know the nature
of the summons, lest they should clamor for a surrender.

But the citizens held a meeting, voted in favor
of non-resistance, and demanded an authentic copy
of the communication, which had been received from
the commander of the English fleet. They adjourned to meet on Monday morning to receive the reply. Governor Stuyvesant was greatly distressed.
After the Sabbath he went to the meeting in person, and endeavored to convince those present of
the impropriety of their demands. But the citizens,

trembling in view of the bombardment of the town, were in no mood to listen to his persuasions.

It was not needful for the English to be in any hurry. The prey was entirely within their grasp. It will be remembered that Governor Winthrop of Hartford, had joined the expedition. Colonel Nicholls addressed a letter to Governor Winthrop, requesting him to visit the city under a flag of truce, and communicate the contents to Governor Stuyvesant. The Dutch governor came out of the fort to receive the letter, and then returned into the fort to read it. The following was the letter:

" MR. WINTHROP :—

" As to those particulars you spoke to me, I do assure you that if the Manhadoes be delivered up to his Majesty, I shall not hinder but any people from the Netherlands may freely come and plant there or thereabouts. And such vessels of their own country, may freely come thither. And any of them may as freely return home, in vessels of their own country; and this and much more is contained in the privilege of his Majesty's English subjects. This much you may, by what means you please, assure the governor from, Sir, your affectionate servant,

RICHARD NICHOLLS."

August 22, 1664. O. S.

The Council demanded that this letter should be exhibited to the people. The governor refused, saying that it would be quite unfavorable to the defence to communicate such intelligence to the inhabitants. As the council persisted, the governor, in a

13*

passion, tore up the letter and trampled it beneath his feet. The rumor spread rapidly that a flag of truce had come.

The citizens collected in a large and excited gathering, and sent a delegation of three persons to demand of the governor the communication which he had received from the hostile fleet. Threats were uttered. Curses were heard. Resistance was declared to be madness. The universal voice clamored for the letter. The community was upon the eve of mutiny.

At length Stuyvesant yielded. A copy of the letter was made out from the fragments, and it was read to the people. This increased their disposition to capitulate. Still the indomitable governor could not endure the thought of surrendering the majestic province of New Netherland to a force of four frigates. He regarded the movement, on the part of the English, as an atrocious act of highway robbery. But he was well aware that there was no escape from the sacrifice.

In the night he sent a vessel, "silently through Hell Gate," to the Directors in Holland, with the following laconic dispatch. "Long Island is gone and lost. The capitol cannot hold out long." When a man's heart is broken his words are few.

Much of the night the governor spent in drawing up a strong remonstrance, in answer to the message of Colonel Nicholls. All the argument was with the Dutch. All the force was with the English. But when argument and force come into collision in this wicked world, argument must generally yield.

In the very able manifesto of the governor, he traced the history of the country from the earliest period to the present time. He deduced the title of the Dutch, to the territory, from the three great principles of Discovery, Settlement, and Purchase from the Indians. He severely denounced the pretence, now put forth by the English, that his, " Britannic Majesty had an indisputable right to all the lands in the north parts of America." Courteously he added that he was confident that if his Majesty had been well informed in the premises, his high sense of justice would have dissuaded him from authorizing the present hostile demonstration. In conclusion he said,

" In case you will act by force of arms, we protest before God and man, that you will perform an act of unjust violence. You will violate the articles of peace solemnly ratified by his Majesty of England, and my Lords the States-General. Again for the prevention of the spilling of innocent blood, not only here but in Europe, we offer you a treaty by our deputies. As regards your threats we have no answer to make, only that we fear nothing but what God may lay upon us. All things are at His disposal, and we can be preserved by Him with small forces as well as by a great army."

CHAPTER XIV.

The Capture of New Amsterdam.

The Approach of the Fleet.—The Governor Unjustly Censured.—The Flag of Truce.—The Haughty Response.—The Remonstrance.—The Defenceless City.—The Surrender.—The Expedition to the Delaware.—Sack and Plunder.—Change of Name.—Testimony to the Dutch Government.—Death of the Governor.—His farm, or Bouwerie.—War Between Holland and England.—New York Menaced by the Dutch.

THE only response which Colonel Nicholls deigned to make to the remonstrance of Governor Stuyvesant, was to put his fleet in motion. A party of soldiers, infantry and cavalry, was landed on Long Island, and they advanced rapidly through the forest, to the little cluster of huts which were scattered along the silent and solitary shores of Brooklyn. These troops were generally volunteers from Connecticut and from the English settlements on Long Island.

The fleet then ascended through the Narrows, and two of the frigates disembarked a number of regular troops just below Brooklyn, to support the volunteers. Two of the frigates, one mounting thirty-six guns, and the other thirty, coming up under full sail, passed directly within range of the guns of the fort, and cast anchor between the fort and Nutten or Governor's Island.

Stuyvesant stood at one of the angles of the fortress as the frigates passed by. It was a critical moment. The fate of the city and the lives of its inhabitants trembled in the balance. The guns were loaded and shotted, and the gunners stood by with their burning matches. A word from the impetuous Stuyvesant would have opened upon the city all the horrors of a bombardment. There were but about twenty guns in the fort. There were sixty-six in the two frigates, whose portholes were opened upon the city; and there were two other frigates just at hand, prepared to bring twenty-eight guns more into the fray.

As Governor Stuyvesant stood at that point, burning with indignation, with the word to fire almost upon his lips, the two clergymen of the place, Messrs. Megapolensis and son, came up and entreated him not to be the first to shed blood in a hopeless conflict. Their persuasions induced the governor to leave the rampart, and intrusting the defence of the fort to fifty men, to take the remainder of the garrison, one hundred in number, to repel if possible, the English, should they attempt a landing. The governor still cherished a faint hope that some accommodation could yet be agreed upon.

The Directors in Holland subsequently, with great severity and, as we think, with great injustice, censured Governor Stuyvesant for his conduct on this occasion. The whole population of the little city was but fifteen hundred. Of them not more than two hundred and fifty were able to bear arms, in addition to the one hundred and fifty regular troops in garrison. And yet the Directors in Holland wrote, in the following cruel terms, to the heroic governor:

" It is an act which can never be justified, that a Director General should stand between the gabions, while the hostile frigates pass the fort, and the mouths of twenty pieces of cannon, and yet give no orders to prevent it. It is unpardonable that he should lend his ear to preachers, and other chicken-hearted persons, demeaning himself as if he were willing to fire, and yet to allow himself to be led in from the bulwark between the preachers. When the frigates had sailed past, he became so troubled that he must then first go out to prevent their landing. The excuse, that it was resolved not to begin hostilities, is very poor, for the English had committed every hostile act."

The governor immediately sent to Colonel

Nicholls a flag of truce conveyed by four of the most distinguished officers of State. Through them he said:

"I feel obliged to defend the city, in obedience to orders. It is inevitable that much blood will be shed on the occurrence of the assault. Cannot some accommodation yet be agreed upon? Friends will be welcome if they come in a friendly manner."

The laconic, decisive and insulting response of Colonel Nicholls was: "I have nothing to do but to execute my mission. To accomplish that I hope to have further conversation with you on the morrow, at the Manhattans. You say that friends will be welcome, if they come in a friendly manner. I shall come with ships and soldiers. And he will be bold indeed who will dare to come on board my ships, to demand an answer or to solicit terms. What then is to be done? Hoist the white flag of surrender, and then something may be considered."

When this imperious message became known it created the greatest consternation throughout the city. Men, women and children flocked to the governor, and, with tears in their eyes, implored him to submit. A brief bombardment would cause the death of hundreds, and would lay the city in ashes. "I had rather," the governor replied, "be carried a corpse to my grave, than to surrender the city."

The civic authority, the clergy and the commanders of the Burgher corps, promptly assembled in the City Hall and drew up the following earnest remonstrance, which was immediately presented to the governor and his council. We give it slightly abbreviated.

"Right Honorable! We, your sorrowful subjects, beg to represent, in these sad circumstances, that having maturely weighed what was necessary to be done, we cannot foresee, for this fort and city of Manhattans, in further resistance, aught else than misery, sorrow, and conflagration; the dishonor of women, the murder of children, and in a word the absolute ruin of fifteen hundred innocent souls, only two hundred and fifty of whom are capable of bearing arms.

"You are aware that four of the English king's frigates are now in the roadstead, with six hundred soldiers on board. They have also commissions to all the governors of New England, a populous and thickly inhabited country, to impress troops, in addition to the forces already on board, for the purpose of reducing New Netherland to his Majesty's obedience.

"These threats we would not have regarded, could we expect the smallest aid. But, God help us, where shall we turn for assistance, to the north

or to the south, to the east or to the west? 'Tis
all in vain. On all sides we are encompassed and
hemmed in by our enemies. If, on the other
hand, we examine our internal strength, alas! it is so
feeble and impotent that unless we ascribe the cir-
cumstance to the mercy of God, we cannot sufficiently express our astonishment that the foe should
have granted us so long a reprieve. He could
have delivered us a prey to the soldiery after one
summons.

"We shall now examine your Honors' fortress.
You know that it is incapable of making head three
days, against so powerful an enemy. Even could
it hold out one, two, three, four, five or six months,
which to our sorrow it cannot do, it is still undeniable that it cannot save the smallest portion of our
entire city, our property and what is dearer to us, our
wives and children, from total ruin. And after considerable bloodshed the fort itself could not be preserved.

"Wherefore, to prevent the aforesaid misfor-
tunes, we humbly, and in bitterness of heart, implore
your Honors not to reject the conditions of so generous a foe, but to be pleased to meet him in the
speediest, best and most reputable manner. Otherwise, which God forbid, we are obliged to protest
before God and the world; and to call down upon
your Honors the vengeance of Heaven for all the
innocent blood which shall be shed in consequence
of your Honors' obstinacy; inasmuch as the commissioners have this day informed us that the English

general has stated that he shall not wait any longer than this day.

"We trust your Honors will not question that to
God, who seeks not the death of the sinner, belongs
obedience rather than to man. We feel certain
that your Honors will exhibit yourselves, in this
pressing exigency and sorrowful season, as men and
christians, and conclude with God's help, an honorable and reasonable capitulation. May the Lord
our God be pleased to grant this to us, Amen"

The above memorial was signed by ninety-four
of the most prominent citizens of New Amsterdam.
One of these signers was the governor's son. All
our readers will perceive that the situation of the
governor had become one of extreme difficulty. A
fleet and army of great strength for the time and
the occasion were before him. This force held in
reserve the whole military power of New England.
The civic officers and citizens of New Amsterdam,
headed by the governor's own son, were loud in
their remonstrance against any defence, and were
almost in a state of mutiny.

The condition of the city was such that the idea
of standing a siege was not for a moment to be
thought of. Along the banks of the North and
East rivers, the village, for the little cluster of three
hundred houses was but a village, was entirely

exposed. Upon the land side, running from river to river, there was a slight fence composed of old and decayed palisades, which scores of years before had been a protection against the savages. In front of this fence there were the remains of a storm-washed breastwork, about three feet high and two feet wide.

The crumbling fort was pronounced by all to be untenable. It was originally constructed as a retreat from the savages, who could only assail it with arrows and hatchets and a few musket balls. It was surrounded by an earthen rampart, about ten feet high and three or four feet thick. In all, there were twenty-four cannons within the enclosure, which was unprotected by any ditch or palisades. In the rear, where the throngs of Broadway now press along, there was a series of forest-crowned eminences whose solitary summits were threaded by an Indian trail. These hills commanded the fort. From their crests the soles of the feet, it was said, of those walking in the squares within, could be seen. There were not five hundred pounds of powder in store fit for use. The gunners declared that a few hours of fighting would exhaust it all. The stock of provisions was equally low, and there was not a well of water within the fort.

It is probable that the majority of common soldiers, in almost any regular army, is composed of

dissolute worthless men.   There are but few persons
but the lost and the reckless who will enlist to spend
their days in shouldering a musket.   A young man
of good character can do better than convert himself
into a part of such a military machine.   The garrison at New Amsterdam was composed of the off-
scouring of Europe.   They were ready to fight
under any banner which would pay them.   They
were eager for the conflict with the English.   At
the first volley they would throw aside their guns
and join the English in the plunder.   One of them
was heard saying to an applauding group:

"Now we hope for a chance to pepper these
devilish Dutch traders.   They have salted us too
long.   We know where their booty is stored.   And
we know also where the young girls live who wear
gold chains."

Under these circumstances the governor was
compelled to yield.   He appointed six commissioners to confer with the same number of the English.
The parties met at Governor Stuyvesant's residence
on his farm or bouwerie, at eight o'clock in the
morning of August 27th.   The terms were speedily
settled, for the English would enforce any demands
which they were disposed to make.   There were
twenty-three articles of agreement, entering into
many details.   The substance was that New Nether-

land passed over entirely to the English. The
Dutch retained their property. If any chose to
leave the country they could do so. The ships of
the Dutch merchants could, for the six months next
ensuing, trade freely with the Netherlands, as heretofore. The people were to be allowed liberty of
conscience in divine worship and church discipline.
No Dutchman should be impressed to serve in war
against any nation whatever. All the inferior civil
officers were allowed to continue in office until
the next election, when they would be required to
take the oath of allegiance to the king of England.

The next day was Sunday. These articles were
therefore not ratified until eight o'clock Monday
morning. It was agreed that within two hours
after the ratification, " the fort and town called New
Amsterdam, upon the island of Manhatoes," should
be delivered up. The military officers of the fort,
and the soldiers were to be permitted to march from
their intrenchments with their arms, drums beating
and colors flying.

Colonel Nicholls took possession of the government. He changed the name of the city from New
Amsterdam to New York, in honor of the Duke of
York, the brother of the King of England. The fort
was called fort James. Colonel Nicholls became

the deputy governor for James, the Duke of York, in administering the affairs of the extended realms which the British government had thus perfidiously seized. We regret to say, but history will bear us out in the assertion, that there is no government in Christendom whose annals are sullied with so many acts of unmitigated villany as the government of Great Britain.

Colonel Nicholls immediately sent an armed force up the river, to take possession of fort Orange; and another to the Delaware, to unfurl the English flag over New Amstel. The name of fort Orange was changed to fort Albany, the second title of the Duke of York. Three frigates were sent to the Delaware. The severest punishment was denounced against the Dutch and Swedes there, should they make any resistance. The same terms were offered them which were granted to the people at New Amsterdam.

The command of this expedition was entrusted to Sir Robert Carr. Notwithstanding the sacred stipulations into which Carr had entered, he trampled them all beneath his feet. Governor Stuyvesant writes,

"At New Amstel, on the South river, notwithstanding they offered no resistance, but demanded good treatment, which however they did not obtain, they were invaded, stript bare, plundered, and many of them sold as slaves in Virginia."

This testimony is corroborated by a London document, which says, "From the city and the inhabitants thereabout were taken one hundred sheep, thirty or forty horses, fifty or sixty cows and oxen, between sixty and seventy negroes, the brew-house still-house and all the material thereunto belonging. The produce of the land, such as corn, hay, etc., was also seized for the king's use, together with the cargo that was unsold, and the bills of what had been disposed of, to the value of four thousand pounds sterling.

"The Dutch soldiers were taken prisoners, and given up to the merchant-man that was there, in payment for his services; and they were transported into Virginia to be sold. All sorts of tools for handicraft tradesmen, and all plough gear, and other things to cultivate the ground, which were in store in great quantity, were likewise seized, together with a sawmill ready to set up, and nine sea buoys with their iron chains.

"Even the inoffensive Menonists, though thoroughly non-combatant from principle, did not escape the sack and plunder to which the whole river was subjected by Carr and his co-marauders. A boat was dispatched to their settlement, which was stripped of everything, even to a very nail."

At New Amsterdam, Colonel Nicholls paid more respect to the terms of the treaty. Citizens, residing there, were not robbed of their private property. But the gentlemen of the West India Company, in Holland, found all their property mercilessly confiscated. Colonel Nicholls seized on everything upon which he could lay his hand. He seemed anxious to eradicate every vestige of the former power. This property was sold at auction that it might thus be distributed among a large number of individual owners. The Colonel shrewdly imagined that he might thus interest all these persons in the maintenance of the new power.

History has but one voice, and that of the severest condemnation, in reference to these transactions on the part of the English government. Mr. O'Callaghan writes :

" Thus was fitly consummated an act of spoliation which, in a period of profound peace, wrested this province from the rightful owners, by violating all public justice and infringing all public law. The only additional outrage that remained was to impose on the country the name of one unknown in history, save as a bigot and a tyrant ; the enemy of religious and political freedom wherever he rul-

14

ed.   New Netherland was accordingly called New York."

Hon. Benjamin F. Butler, in his outline of the State of New York writes, "In the history of the royal ingrates by whom it was planned and for whose benefit it was perpetrated, there are few acts more base, none more characteristic."

Mr. Brodhead, in his admirable History of the State of New York, says, " The flag of England was, at length, triumphantly displayed where for half a century that of Holland had triumphantly waved ; and from Virginia to Canada, the king of Great Britain was acknowledged as sovereign.   Whatever may have been its ultimate consequences, this treacherous and violent seizure of the territory and possessions of an unsuspecting ally, was no less a breach of private justice than of public faith.   It may indeed be affirmed that, among all the acts of selfish perfidy which royal ingratitude conceived and executed, there have been few more character- istic and none more base."

Thus the Dutch dominion in North America passed forever away.   I cannot refrain from quoting the just tribute to the Dutch government contained in Mr. Brodhead's History.   " Holland," he writes, " has long been the theme for the ridicule of British writers ; and even in this country the character and manners of the Dutch have been made the subjects of an unworthy depreciation. Yet, without under-valuing others, it may confidently be claimed that, to no nation in the world is the Republic of the West more indebted than to the United Provinces, for the idea of the confederation of sovereign States; for noble principles of constitutional free-dom; for magnanimous sentiments of religious toler-ation; for characteristic sympathy with subjects of oppression; for liberal doctrines in trade and com-merce; for illustrious patterns of public integrity and private virtue, and for generous and timely aid in the establishment of independence. Nowhere among the people of the United States can men be found excelling in honesty, industry, courtesy or accomplishment, the posterity of the early Dutch settlers of New Netherland."

Soon after the surrender, Governor Stuyvesant was recalled to Europe to vindicate his conduct. The severest charges were brought against him. He addressed to the States-General an "Account of the Circumstances preceding the surrender of New Netherland." It was a triumphant vindication of his conduct. But the unfortunate are rarely treated with justice. The pride of Holland was deeply touched by the loss of its North American posses-sions. Governor Stuyvesant soon returned to New

York, and lived in much seclusion in his spacious house on his farm, until he died, in the year 1672. The governor's remains were entombed at his chapel in the Bouwery, now St. Mark's Church.

There were two roads which led from the fort at the Battery, to the northern part of the island. One of these followed along the present line of Broadway to what is now the Park, which was at that time a large unenclosed open field far out of town called the Common. The road then wound along by the southeastern side of the common and by the line of Chatham street and the Bouwery out to Harlaem. This became eventually the "Old Post Road" to Boston. Governor Stuyvesant's Bouwery consisted of many acres of land. The farm embraced the land in the region of Third avenue and Thirteenth street. In the spring of 1647, a pear tree was planted upon this spot, which was long known as "Stuyvesant's pear tree." For more than two centuries it continued to bear fruit. In its latter years, this venerable relic of the past was cherished with the utmost care. It presented many touching indications of its extreme old age. In its two hundred and twentieth year it bloomed for the last time. "Since the fall of the tree," writes Mr. Stone, "a promising shoot from the ancient stock has taken its place, and shows a hardy vigor which may yet enable it to rival its progenitor in age."

In the year 1665, the year which followed the capture of the city, war broke out between England and Holland. It was then generally expected that the States of Holland would make an attempt to recover the lost territory of New Netherland. It was rumored that De Ruyter, one of the Dutch Admirals, had actually set sail, with a large squadron, for New York. The rumor caused great commotion in the city. The national spirit of the Dutch residents was roused to intensity. De Ruyter had indeed sailed with the object of recapturing the province.

Colonel Nicholls was a man of great energy. He immediately commenced with all vigor, the work of repairing the crumbling fortifications, and of erecting new ones. But he found none to co-operate heartily with him, save the few English soldiers, whose bayonets held the conquered province in subjection. A meeting of all the Dutch inhabitants was called to ascertain the tone of public sentiment, and to endeavor to inspire the community with some enthusiasm for the defence.

But no enthusiasm was elicited. The Dutch were not at all unwilling that their countrymen should come back and reclaim their own. Even to

defend themselves from the humiliation of conquest, by their English assailants, they had not
been willing to submit to a bombardment. Much
less were they now willing to subject themselves
to the horrors of war, when the flag of Holland was
approaching for their deliverance. They did not
venture however, openly to oppose the ruler whom
the fortunes of war had set over them, or to express
sympathy for the success of the approaching fleet,
which might be pronounced treason, and might expose them to severe punishment.

They contented themselves with manifesting entire indifference, or in offering sundry excuses.
They very sensibly assumed the ground that they
were a feeble defenceless colony, far away in the
wilderness, entirely unable to cope with the forces
which the great maritime powers of England or Holland might send against them. When an English
fleet opened the portholes of its broadsides upon
their little village, they could do nothing but surrender. Should a fleet from Holland now anchor in
their waters they must let events take their natural
course.

Colonel Nicholls, as governor, had gifts of honor
and opulence in his hands. As was to have been
expected, there were a few Dutch citizens who were
eager to gratify the governor by co-operating with

him in all his plans. This number, however, was small. The great mass of the citizens assumed an air of indifference, while, in heart, they longed for the appearance of the Dutch fleet in such strength as to render resistance impossible.

But either the storms of the ocean, or some other engagements, arrested the progress of the squadron, until after the rupture between England and Holland was temporarily healed. Colonel Nicholls remained in command at New York about four years. His administration was as popular as could reasonably have been expected under the circumstances. He gradually relaxed the severity of his rule, and wisely endeavored to promote the prosperity of the colony. The conquest had retarded the tide of emigration from Holland, and had given a new impulse to that from England. The Dutch gradually became reconciled to his rule. They enjoyed all the rights and immunities which were conferred upon any of the subjects of England in her American colonies. Out of respect to the governor they organized two militia companies, the officers of which were from the most distinguished of the Dutch citizens, and they received their commissions from him.

In August of 1668, Colonel Nicholls, at his own request, was recalled, and he returned to England.

The Dutch did not love him, for they never could forget the circumstances under which he had conquered their province. But he had won their respect. As he embarked for the shores of England the great body of the citizens complimented him by a respectful leave-taking.

Colonel Nicholls was succeeded in the government of the province, by Colonel Francis Lovelace. He was an English officer of respectable abilities, and of worthy character. Under his sway, New York for five years, until 1673, enjoyed prosperity and peace. New agitations then took place.

The peace, of which we have spoken, between England and Holland, was of but transient duration. In 1672 war was again declared by England. The conflict which ensued was mainly upon the ocean. New York had so grown since its conquest by the English, and could so easily be reinforced by almost any number of men from populous New England, that the Dutch did not think that there was any chance of their then being able to regain the colony. They, however, fitted out a fleet of five ships, to cruise along the coast of North America, destroy the English, and inflict such injury upon any and all of the English colonies as might be in their power.

Governor Lovelace had no idea that any Dutch

ships would venture through the Narrows. He made no special effort to strengthen the defences of New York. Early in February he went to Westchester county, to visit at the residence of his friend Mr. Pell. This was quite a journey in those days. The command of the fort was entrusted, during his absence to Captain John Manning.

A vessel entered the port, bringing the intelligence that a Dutch fleet had been seen off the coast of Virginia, sailing in the direction of New York. This created great commotion. A dispatch was sent, in the utmost haste, to the governor, summoning his return. He promptly mustered, for the defence, all the forces he could raise in the city and neighboring counties, and soon five hundred armed men were parading the streets of New York.

It proved a false dream. No enemy appeared. The troops were disbanded. They returned to their homes. The community was lulled into a very false sense of security. In July, the governor again was absent, on a visit to Connecticut. On the 29th of July the Dutch fleet appeared at Sandy Hook, and, learning from some of the inhabitants of Long Island, whose sympathies were still cordially with the fatherland, that the city was entirely defenceless and could easily be taken, ventured to try the experiment. They had not approached the bay with

14*

any such design. They had supposed their force
entirely inadequate for so important a capture. The
fleet quietly sailed up the bay and, as the English
fleet had done but a few years before, anchored opposite the Battery, and turned their broadsides towards the city.

Colonel Manning sent a hurried despatch to the
governor, who could by no possibility return for several days, and fluttered about in the attempt to
beat up recruits. But no recruits were forthcom-
ing. The sight of the flag of Holland, again triumphantly floating in the harbor, was joyful to
many eyes.

The great majority of the people, in the city and
in the country, were of Dutch descent. Consequently the recruiting parties which were raised, were in
no mood to peril their lives in defence of the flag of
England. Indeed it is said that one party of the
recruits marched to the Battery and deliberately
spiked several of the guns, opposite the City-hall.

It was a most singular revolution of the wheel
of fortune. Captain Manning had but fifty soldiers
within the fort. None of these were willing to fight.
One-half of them were such raw recruits that captain Manning said that they had never put their
heads over the ramparts. A few broadsides from
the Dutch fleet would dismount every gun in the

fort, and put to flight all the defenders who should survive the volley.   This was alike obvious to the assailants and the assailed.

CHAPTER XV.

The Final Surrender.

The Summons.—The Bombardment.—Disembarkation of the Land
Force.—Indecision of Captain Manning.—The Surrender.—
Short Administration of the Dutch.—Social Customs.—The Tea
Party.—Testimony of Travellers.—Visit to Long Island.—
Fruitfulness of the Country.—Exploration of Manhattan Island.

THE Dutch ships, having anchored and prepared
themselves for the immediate opening of the bombardment, a boat was sent on shore with a flag of
truce, to demand the surrender of the city. At the
same time a boat was sent by Colonel Manning,
from the fort to the ships. The boats passed each
other without any interchange of words. Colonel
Manning's boat bore simply the message to the
Dutch Admirals, " Why do you come in such a hostile manner to disturb his Majesty's subjects in this
place?" As England and Holland were then engaged in open war, one would hardly think that such
an inquiry was then called for. When Colonel
Nicholls came to New Amsterdam with his English
fleet, the two nations were in friendly alliance.

Such a question then would have been very appropriate.

The boat from the Dutch fleet bore a flag of truce at its stern, and was accompanied by a trumpeter, who asked for the English officer in command and presented the following message to Colonel Manning:

"The force of war, now lying in your sight, is sent by the High and Mighty States-General and his serene Highness the Prince of Orange, for the purpose of destroying their enemies. We have sent you therefore, this letter, together with our trumpeter, to the end that, upon the sight hereof, you surrender unto us the fort called James, promising good quarter; or by your refusal we shall be obliged to proceed, both by land and water, in such manner as we shall find to be most advantageous for the High and Mighty States."

Captain Manning returned an answer simply acknowledging the receipt of the message, and informing the Dutch Admirals that he had already dispatched officers to communicate with him. He promised upon the return of those messengers to give a definite reply to his summons.

The Dutch Admirals, Benckes and Evertson, were not disposed to waste any time in parleying. They probably remembered the circumstances under

which the province of New Netherland had been
wrested from them by its present possessors, and
they rejoiced that the hour of retribution had thus
unexpectedly come.

They therefore sent back word that their batteries were loaded and shotted and ready to open
fire; that one half hour and one half hour only,
would be granted for deliberation; that immediately
upon the arrival of the boat at the fort the half
hour glass would be turned up; and that if, when
its last sands fell, the white flag of surrender were
not raised upon the fort, the bombardment would be
commenced.

The last sands fell and no white flag appeared.
Instantly the thunder of a cannon echoed over the
bay, and a storm of iron hail came crashing upon
the frail fort, killing and wounding a number of men.
Volley after volley succeeded without any intermis-
sion. Captain Manning made no attempt to return
the fire. He and his powerless garrison hurried to
places of safety, leaving the ramparts to be ploughed
up and the barracks to be battered down without
any resistance.

While this cannonade was going on, the Dutch
Admirals manned their boats with a land force of
six hundred men, and they were disembarked upon
the shore of the island without encountering any

foe. The little band of English soldiers was powerless, and the Dutch inhabitants were much more
disposed to welcome their countrymen as deliverers
than to oppose them as enemies. These Dutch
troops were armed with hand grenades and such
other weapons as were deemed necessary to take
the place by storm. Rapidly they marched through
the fields to the Common, now called the Park. It
was, as we have mentioned, nearly a mile north from
the fort.

Here they formed in column to march upon
the town, under their leader, Captain Colve. The
English commander, Captain Manning, sent three
of his subordinate officers, without any definite
message, to Captain Colve, to talk over the question
of a capitulation. It would seem that Captain Manning was quite incompetent for the post he occupied.
He was bewildered and knew not what to do. As
his envoys had no proposals to make, two of them
were detained and held under the Dutch standard,
while the third, Captain Carr, was sent back to
inform the English commander that if in one quarter of an hour the place were not surrendered, it
would be taken by storm. In the meantime the
troops were put upon the march.

Captain Carr, aware of the indecision of Captain
Manning and of the personal peril he, as an English-

man, would encounter, with six hundred Dutch
soldiers sweeping the streets, burning with the desire
to avenge past wrongs, did not venture back into
the town with his report, but fled into the interior
of the island. The troops pressed on to the head
of Broadway, where a trumpeter was sent forward
to receive the answer to the summons which it was
supposed had been made. He speedily returned,
saying that the commander of the fort had, as yet,
obtained no answer from the commissioners he had
sent to receive from the Dutch commander his
propositions.

Captain Colve supposed that he was trifled with.
Indignantly he exclaimed " They are not to play the
fool with us in this way, forward march." With
the beat of drums and trumpet peals and waving
banners his solid columns marched down the Broadway road to the little cluster of about three hundred
houses, at the extreme southern point of the island.
An army of six hundred men at that time and place
presented a very imposing and terrible military
array. In front of his troops the two commissioners
who had been detained, were marched under guard.

As they approached the fort, Captain Manning
sent another flag of truce to the Dutch commander,
with the statement that he was ready to surrender
the fort with all its arms and ammunition, if the

officers and soldiers were permitted to march out with their private property and to the music of their band. These terms were acceded to. The English troops, with no triumphal strains, vacated the fort. The Dutch banners soon waved from the ramparts, cheered by the acclaim of the conquerors.

Captain Manning was, in his turn, as severely censured by the people of the English colonies in America, and by the home government, as Governor Stuyvesant had been on the day of his misfortune. English pride was grievously mortified, that the commandant of an English fort should allow himself to be fired upon for hours without returning a shot.

The unfortunate captain was subsequently tried by court-martial for cowardice and treachery. He was condemned. His sword was broken over his head and he was declared incompetent forever to hold any station of trust or authority under the government. Governor Lovelace was condemned for neglect of duty. He received a severe reprimand, and all his property was confiscated to the Duke of York.

The victorious Dutch commanders appointed Captain Colve as governor of recaptured New Netherland. With great energy he commenced his rule. The name of New York was changed to New

Orange, and fort James became fort Hendrick.
Work was immediately commenced upon the fortifications, and large sums of money were expended
upon them, so that within two months they were
deemed so strong that it was thought that no
English fleet would dare to venture within range
of their guns. The whole city assumed the aspect
of a military post. Nearly every citizen was trained
to arms. The Common, now the Park, was the pa-
rade ground where the troops were daily drilled. It
was very firmly resolved that the city should not
again surrender without the firing of a gun.

The municipal institutions were all re-organized
to conform to those of the fatherland. This second
administration of the Dutch was of but short duration. On the 9th of January, 1674, but about three
months after the re-capture of the city, a treaty of
peace was signed between England and Holland.
The sixth article of this treaty read as follows,

"Whatsoever countries, islands, ports, towns,
castles or forts have been taken on both sides, since
the time that the late unhappy war broke out, either
in Europe or elsewhere, shall be restored to the
former lord or proprietor in the same condition they
shall be in when peace itself shall be proclaimed."

Several months however transpired before the
actual re-surrender of the city to the English. On

the 10th of November, 1674, a little more than one
year after the capture of the city by the Dutch,
this change took place. Mr. David V. Valentine
writes :

"This event was not distasteful to the great
body of the citizens, whose national sentiment had,
in a measure, given way before the obvious
advantages to their individual interests of having a settled authority established over them,
with the additional privilege of English institutions which were then considered of a liberal ten-
dency."

In conclusion, we have but a few words to say
respecting the manners and customs in the thriving
little village of New York, in these primitive days.
People were then, to say the least, as happy as they
are now. Food was abundant, and New York was
far-famed for its cordial hospitality. Days of recre-
ation were more abundant than now. The principal
social festivals were " quilting," "apple paring,"
and "husking." Birthdays, christenings, and mar-
riage anniversaries were also celebrated with much
festivity. Upon most of these occasions there was
abundant feasting. Dancing was the favorite amusement, with which the evening was almost invariably
terminated. In this busy community the repose of
the night was necessary to prepare for the labors of

the ensuing day. The ringing of the nine o'clock
bell was the signal for all to retire.

A mild form of negro slavery existed in those
days. The slaves danced to the music of their rude
instruments in the markets. The young men and
maidens often met on the Bowling green and danced
around the May pole. Turkey shooting was a favorite amusement, which usually took place on the
Common. New Year's Day was devoted to the interchange of visits. Every door was thrown open,
and all guests were welcome, friends as well as
strangers, as at a Presidential levee. This custom
of olden time has passed down to us from our worthy Dutch predecessors. Dinner parties were unknown. But tea-parties, with the ladies, were very
common.

"To take tea out," writes Mr. William L. Stone,
in his interesting History of New York, "was a
Dutch institution, and one of great importance.
The matrons, arrayed in their best petticoats and lin-
sey jackets, home-spun by their own wheels, would
proceed on the intended afternoon visit. They wore
capacious pockets, with scissors, pin-cushion and
keys hanging from their girdle, outside of their
dress; and reaching the neighbor's house the visitors industriously used knitting needles and tongues
at the same time. The village gossip was talked

over; neighbors' affairs settled, and the stockings finished by tea-time, when the important meal appeared on the table, precisely at six o'clock.

"This was always the occasion for the display of the family plate, with the Lilliputian cups, of rare old family china, out of which the guests sipped the fragrant herb. A large lump of loaf sugar invariably accompanied each cup, on a little plate, and the delightful beverage was sweetened by an occasional nibble, amid the more solid articles of waffles and Dutch doughnuts. The pleasant visit finished, the visitors donning cloaks and hoods, as bonnets were unknown, proceeded homeward in time for milking and other necessary household duties.

"The kitchen fire-places were of immense size, large enough to roast a whole sheep. The hooks and trammels sustained large iron pots and kettles. In the spacious chimney-corners the children and negroes gathered, telling stories and cracking nuts by the blazing pine-knots, while the industrious *vrows* turned the merry spinning-wheel, and their lords, the worthy burghers, mayhap just returned from an Indian scrimmage, quietly smoked their long pipes, as they sat watching the wreaths curling above their heads. At length the clock with its brazen tongue having proclaimed the hour of nine, family prayers were said, and all retired, to rise with the dawn."

In the summer of 1679, but five years after the
final accession of New Netherland by the English,
two gentlemen from Holland, as the committee of a
religious sect, visited the Hudson river, to report
respecting the condition of the country, and to select a suitable place for the establishment of a colony. They kept a minute journal of their daily adventures. From their narrative one can obtain a
very vivid picture of New York life two hundred
years ago.

On Saturday, the 23d day of September, they
landed at New York, and found it a very strange
place. A fellow passenger, whose name was Ger-
ritt, and who was on his return from Europe, resided
in New York. He took the travellers to the house
of one of his friends, where they were regaled with
very luscious peaches, and apples far better than
any they had seen in Holland. They took a walk
out into the fields and were surprised to see how
profusely the orchards were laden with fruit. They
took up lodgings with the father-in-law of their fel-
low-traveller, and in the evening were regaled with
rich milk. The next day was Sunday.

"We walked awhile," they write, "in the pure
mountain air, along the margin of the clear running
water of the sea, which is driven up this river at
every tide. We went to church and found truly

there a wild worldly people. I say wild, not only
because the people are wild, as they call it in Europe, but because most all the people who go there,
partake somewhat of the nature of the country; that
is peculiar to the land where they live."

The preacher did not please them. "He used
such strange gestures and language," writes one of
them, "that I think I never in my life heard anything
more miserable. As it is not strange in these countries, to have men as ministers, who drink, we could
imagine nothing else than that he had been drinking
a little this morning. His text was *Come unto me
all ye, etc.;* but he was so rough that the rough-
est and most godless of our sailors were astonished.

"The church being in the fort, we had an opportunity to look through the latter, as we had come
too early for preaching. The fort is built upon the
point formed by the two rivers, namely the East
river, which is the water running between the Manhattans and Long Island, and the North river,
which runs straight up to fort Orange. In front of
the fort there is a small island called Nut Island.
Around the point of this vessels must sail in going
out or in, whereby they are compelled to pass close
by the point of the fort, where they can be flanked
by several of the batteries. It has only one gate

and that is on the land side, opening upon a broad lane or street, called the Broadway."

They went to church again in the afternoon. "After preaching," they write, "the good old people with whom we lodged, who, indeed if they were not the best on all the Manhattan, were at least among the best, especially the wife, begged we would go with their son Gerrit, to one of their daughters who lived in a delightful place and kept a tavern, where we would be able to taste the beer of New Netherland. So we went, for the purpose of seeing what was to be seen. But when we arrived there we were much deceived. On account of its being, to some extent, a pleasant spot, it was resorted to on Sundays by all sorts of revellers and was a low pothouse. It being repugnant to our feelings to be there, we walked into the orchard, to seek pleasure in contemplating the innocent objects of nature. A great storm of rain coming up in the evening, we retraced our steps in the dark, exploring our way through a salt meadow, and over water upon the trunk of a tree."

On Thursday the 26th, our two travellers, at two o'clock in the afternoon, crossed East river to visit Long Island. The fare in the ferry-boat, which was rowed across, was three stivers, less than half a cent of our money, for each person. They climbed the hill and walked along through an open road and a little woods to " the first village, called Breukelen, which has a small and ugly little church in the middle of the road." The island was then mostly inhabited by Indians. There were several flourishing farms in the vicinity of Brooklyn, which they visited and where they were bountifully regaled with milk, cider, fruit, tobacco and " first and most of all, miserable rum, brought from Barbadoes, and which is called by the Dutch *kill devil.*"

The peach orchards were breaking down beneath the burden of luscious fruit. They often could not step without trampling upon the peaches, and yet the trees were full as they could bear. Though the swine were fattened upon them, still large numbers perished upon the ground. In the evening they went on to a place called Gouanes, where they were very hospitably entertained. It was a chill evening, and they found a brilliant fire of hickory wood crackling upon the hearth.

" There had already been thrown upon it," they write, " a pail full of Gouanes oysters, which are the best in the country. They are large, some of them not less than a foot long, and they grow, sometimes ten, twelve and sixteen together, and are then like a piece of rock. We had for supper a roasted haunch of venison which weighed thirty pounds, and which he had bought of the Indians for fifteen cents. The meat was exceedingly tender and good and quite fat. We were served also with wild turkey, which was also fat and of a good flavor, and a wild goose. Everything we had was the natural production of the country. We saw lying in a heap, a hill of watermelons as large as pumpkins. It was late at night when we went to rest, in a Kermis bed, as it is called, in the corner of the hearth, alongside of a good fire."

The next morning they threaded their way through the forest, and along the shore to the extreme west end of the island, where fort Hamilton now stands. They passed through a large plantation, of the Najack Indians, which was waving with corn. A noise of pounding drew them to a place where a very aged Indian woman was beating beans out of the pods with a stick, which she did with amazing dexterity. Near by was the little cluster of houses of the dwindling tribe. The village consisted of seven or eight huts, occupied by between twenty and thirty Indians, men, women and children.

These huts were about sixty feet long and fifteen wide. The floor was of earth. The posts were large limbs of trees, planted firmly in the ground. The sides were of reeds and the bark of trees. An open

space, about six inches wide, ran along the whole
length of the roof, for the passage of smoke. On
the sides the roof was so low that a man could not
stand under it.

"They build their fire in the middle of the floor,
according to the number of families which live in
the hut ; not only the families themselves, but each
Indian alone, according as he is hungry, at all hours
morning, noon and night. They lie upon mats with
their feet towards the fire. All in one house, are
generally of one stock, as father and mother, with
their offspring. Their bread is maize, pounded by a
stone, which is mixed with water and baked under
the hot ashes."

"They gave us a small piece when we entered ;
and although the grains were not ripe, and it was
half-baked and coarse grains, we nevertheless had to
eat it, or at least not throw it away before them,
which they would have regarded as a great sin, or
a great affront. We chewed a little of it with long
teeth, and managed to hide it so that they did not
see it."

On Wednesday a farmer harnessed his horse
to a wagon and carried them back to the city.
The road led through the forest and over very rough
and stony hills, making the ride quite uncomfortable. Passing again through the little village of

Breukelen, they crossed the ferry and reached home about noon. On Friday they took an exploring tour through the island of Manhattan. Their pleasant description is worth transcribing.

"This island is about seven hours distance in length, but it is not a full hour broad. The sides are indented with bays, coves and creeks. It is almost entirely taken up, that is the land is held by private owners, but not half of it is cultivated. Much of it is good woodland. The west end, on which the city lies, is entirely cleared, for more than an hour's distance, though that is the poorest ground; the best being on the east and north side. There are many brooks of fresh water running through it, pleasant and proper for man and beast to drink; as well as agreeable to behold, affording cool and.pleasant resting places, but especially suitable places for the construction of mills, for though there is no overflow of water, it can be used.

"A little east of New Harlaem, there are two ridges of very high rocks, with a considerable space between them, displaying themselves very majestically, and inviting all men to acknowledge in them the grandeur, power and glory of the Creator, who has impressed such marks upon them. Between them runs the road to *Spuyt den Duyvel.* The one to the north is the most apparent. The south ridge is

covered with earth on its north side, but it can be
seen from the water or from the mainland beyond
to the south. The soil between these ridges is very
good, though a little hilly and stony. It would be
very suitable, in my opinion, for planting vineyards,
in consequence of its being shut off on both sides,
from the winds which would most injure them; and
it is very warm. We found blue grapes along the
road; which were very good and sweet, and as good
as any I have tasted in the fatherland.

"We went from the city, following the Broadway,
over the valley or the fresh water. Upon both sides
of this way there were many habitations of negroes,
mulattoes and whites. The negroes were formerly
the slaves of the West India Company. But, in
consequence of the frequent changes and conquests
of the country, they have obtained their freedom,
and settled themselves down where they thought
proper, and thus on this road, where they have grown
enough to live on with their families. We left the
village called Bowery on the right hand, and went
through the woods to Harlaem, a tolerably large
village situated directly opposite the place where the
northeast creek and the East river come together.
It is about three hours' journey from New Amsterdam."

From the account which these gentlemen give,

the morals of the people certainly do not appear to have been essentially better than now. They passed the night at the house of the sheriff. "This house was constantly filled with people all the time drinking, for the most part, that execrable rum. He had also the best cider we have tasted. Among the crowd we found a person of quality, an Englishman, named Captain Carteret, whose father is in great favor with the king. The king has given his father, Sir George Carteret, the entire government of the lands west of the North river in New Netherland, with power to appoint as governor whom he pleases.

"This son is a very profligate person. He married a merchant's daughter here, and has so lived with his wife that her father has been compelled to take her home again. He runs about among the farmers and stays where he can find most to drink, and sleeps in barns on the straw. If he conducted himself properly, he could be, not only governor here, but hold higher positions, for he has studied the moralities and seems to have been of a good understanding. But that is all now drowned. His father, who will not acknowledge him as his son, allows him yearly as much only as is necessary for him to live on."

Saturday morning they set out from Harlaem village to go to the northern extremity of the island.

" Before we left we did not omit supplying ourselves with peaches, which grew in an orchard along the road. The whole ground was covered with them and with apples lying upon the new grain with which the orchard was planted. The peaches were the most delicious we had yet eaten. We proceeded on our way and when we were not far from the point of *Spuyt den Duyvel,* we could see on our left the rocky cliffs of the mainland, and on the other side of the North river these cliffs standing straight up and down, with the grain just as if they were antimony.

" We crossed over the *Spuyt den Duyvel* in a canoe, and paid nine stivers fare for us three, which was very dear.* We followed the opposite side of the land and came to the house of one Valentyn. He had gone to the city; but his wife was so much rejoiced to see Hollanders that she hardly knew what to do for us. She set before us what she had. We left after breakfasting there. Her son showed us the way, and we came to a road entirely covered with peaches. We asked a boy why he let them lie there and why he did not let the hogs eat them. He answered 'We do not know what to do with them, there are so many. The hogs are satiated with them and will not eat any more.'

* This was one cent and a half for the three, or half a cent each.

"We pursued our way now a small distance, through the woods and over the hills, then back again along the shore to a point where an Englishman lived, who was standing ready to cross over. He carried us over with him and refused to take any pay for our passage, offering us at the same time, some of his rum, a liquor which is everywhere. We were now again at Harlaem, and dined with the sheriff, at whose house we had slept the night before. It was now two o'clock. Leaving there, we crossed over the island, which takes about three-quarters of an hour to do, and came to the North river. We continued along the shore to the city, where we arrived in the evening, much fatigued, having walked this day about forty miles."

The rather singular record for the next day, which was Sunday, was as follows: "We went at noon to-day to hear the English minister, whose service took place after the Dutch service was out. There were not above twenty-five or thirty people in the church. The first thing that occurred was the reading of all their prayers and ceremonies out of the prayer-book, as is done in all Episcopal churches. A young man then went into the pulpit, and commenced preaching, who thought he was performing wonders. But he had a little book in his hand, out of which he read his sermon which was about quarter of an hour or half an hour long. With this the services were concluded; at which we could not be sufficiently astonished."

Though New York had passed over to British rule, still for very many years the inhabitants remained Dutch in their manners, customs and modes of thought. There was a small stream, emptying into the East river nearly opposite Blackwell's Island. This stream was crossed by a bridge which was called Kissing Bridge. It was a favorite drive, for an old Dutch custom entitled every gentleman to salute his lady with a kiss as he crossed.

The town wind-mill stood on a bluff within the present Battery. Pearl street at that time formed the river bank. Both Water street and South street have been reclaimed from the river. The city wall consisted of a row of palisades, with an embankment nine feet high. Upon the bastions of this rampart several cannon were mounted.

15*

CHAPTER XVI.

The Olden Time.

Wealth and Rank of the Ancient Families.—Their Vast Landed Estates.—Distinctions in Dress.—Veneration for the Patroon.— Kip's Mansion.—Days of the Revolution.—Mr. John Adams' Journal.— Negro Slavery.— Consequences of the System.— General Panic.

MANY of the families who came from the Old World to the Hudson when New Netherland was under the Dutch regime, brought with them the tokens of their former rank and affluence. Valuable paintings adorned their walls. Rich plate glittered upon their dining table. Obsequious servants, who had been accustomed in feudal Europe to regard their masters as almost beings of a superior order, still looked up to them in the same reverential service. The social distinctions of the old country very soon began to prevail in the thriving village of New York. The governor was fond of show and was fully aware of its influence upon the popular mind. His residence became the seat of quite a genteel little court.

"The country was parcelled out," writes Rev. Bishop Kip, "among great proprietors. We can trace them from the city of New Amsterdam to the northern part of the State. In what is now the thickly populated city were the lands of the Stuyvesants, originally the *Bouwerie* of the old governor. Next above were the grant to the Kip family, called Kip's Bay, made in 1638. In the centre of the island was the possessions of the De Lanceys. Opposite, on Long Island, was the grant of the Laurence family. We cross over Harlaem river and reach Morrisania, given to the Morris family. Beyond this on the East river, was De Lancey's farm, another grant to that powerful family; while on the Hudson to the west, was the lower Van Courtland manor, and the Phillipse manor. Above, at Peekskill, was the upper manor of the Van Courtlands. Then came the manor of Kipsburg, purchased by the Kip family from the Indians in 1636, and made a royal grant by governor Dongan two years afterwards.

"Still higher up was the Van Rensselaer manor, twenty-four miles by forty-eight; and above that the possession of the Schuylers. Farther west, on the Mohawk, were the broad lands of Sir William Johnson, created a baronet for his services in the

old French and Indian wars, who lived in a rude
magnificence at Johnson Hall."

"The very names of places in some cases show
their history. Such for instance, is that of Yonkers.
The word *Younker*, in the languages of northern
Europe, means the nobly born, the gentleman. In
Westchester, on the Hudson river, still stands the
old manor house of the Phillipse family. The writer
remembers in his early days when visiting there, the
large rooms and richly ornamented ceilings, with
quaint old formal gardens about the house. When
before the revolution, Mr. Phillipse lived there, lord
of all he surveyed, he was always spoken of by his
tenantry as the Yonker, the gentleman, *par excel-
lence*. In fact he was the only person of social rank
in that part of the country. In this way the town,
which subsequently grew up about the old manor
house, took the name of Yonkers.

The early settlement of New England was very
different in its character. Nearly all the emigrants
were small farmers, upon social equality, cultivating
the fields with their own hands. Governors Carver
and Bradford worked as diligently with hoe and
plough as did any of their associates. They were
simply first among equals.

"The only exception to this," writes Mr. Kip,
" which we can remember was the case of the Gardi-

ners of Maine. Their wide lands were confiscated
for their loyalty. But on account of some informal-
ity, after the Revolution, they managed to recover
their property and are still seated at Gardiner."

For more than a century these distinguished
families in New Netherland retained their supremacy undisputed. They filled all the posts of honor
and emolument. The distinctions in society were
plainly marked by the dress. The costume of the
gentleman was very rich. His coat of glossy velvet
was lined with gold lace. His flowing sleeves and
ruffled cuffs gave grace to all the movements of his
arms and hands. Immense wigs adorned his brow
with almost the dignity of Olympian Jove. A glittering rapier, with its embossed and jewelled scab-
bard, hung by his side.

The common people in New Netherland, would
no more think of assuming the dress of a gentleman
or lady, than with us, a merchant or mechanic would
think of decorating himself in the dress of a Major-
General in the United States army. There was an
impassable gulf between the peasantry and the aris-
tocracy. The laborers on these large Dutch estates
were generally poor peasants, who had been brought
over by the landed proprietors, passage free. They
were thus virtually for a number of years, slaves of
the *patroon*, serving him until, by their labor, they

had paid for their passage money. In the language of the day they were called Redemptioners. Often the term of service of a man, who had come over with his family, amounted to seven years.

"This system," writes Mr. Kip, "was carried out to an extent of which most persons are ignorant. On the Van Rensselaer manor, there were at one time, several thousand tenants, and their gathering was like that of the Scottish clans. When a member of the family died they came down to Albany to do honor at the funeral, and many were the hogsheads of good ale which were broached for them. They looked up to the *Patroon* with a reverence which was still lingering in the writer's early day, notwithstanding the inroads of democracy. And before the Revolution this feeling was shared by the whole country. When it was announced, in New York, a century ago, that the Patroon was coming down from Albany by land, the day he was expected to reach the city, crowds turned out to see him enter in his coach and four.

The aristocratic Dutchmen cherished a great contempt for the democratic Puritans of New England. One of the distinguished members of a colonial family in New York, who died in the year 1740, inserted the following clause in his will :

" It is my wish that my son may have the best

education that is to be had in England or America.
But my express will and directions are, that he
never be sent for that purpose, to the Connecticut
colonies, lest he should imbibe in his youth, that
low craft and cunning, so incidental to the people
of that country, which is so interwoven in their con-
stitutions, that all their acts cannot disguise it from
the world ; though many of them, under the sancti-
fied garb of religion, have endeavored to impose
themselves on the world as honest men."

Usually once in a year the residents in their imposing manorial homes repaired, from their rural re-
treats, to New York to make their annual purchases. After the country passed into the hands of the
English, several men of high families came over.
These all held themselves quite aloof from the
masses of the people. And there was no more
disposition among the commonalty to claim equality
with these high-born men and dames, than there
was in England for the humble farmers to deny
any social distinction between themselves and the
occupants of the battlemented castles which overshadowed the peasant's lowly cot.

Lord Cornbury was of the blood royal. The
dress and etiquette of courts prevailed in his spacious saloons. "About many of their old country
houses," writes Mr. Kip, " were associations gather-

ed often coming down from the first settlement of
the country, giving them an interest which can
never invest the new residences of those whom later times elevated through wealth. Such was the
Van Courtland manor-house, with its wainscotted
room and guest chamber; the Rensselaer manor-
house, where of old had been entertained Talley-
rand, and the exiled princes from Europe; the
Schuyler house, so near the Saratoga battle-field,
and marked by memories of that glorious event
in the life of its owner; and the residence of
the Livingstons, on the banks of the Hudson,
of which Louis Philippe expressed such grateful recollections when, after his elevation to the
throne, he met, in Paris, the son of his former
host."

At Kip's Bay there was a large mansion which
for two centuries attracted the admiration of behold-
ers. It was a large double house with the addition
of a wing. From the spacious hall, turning to the
left, you entered the large dining-saloon. The two
front windows gave you a view of the beautiful bay.
The two rear windows opened upon a pleasant rural
landscape. In this dining-room a large dinner party
was held, in honor of Andre the day before he set
out upon his fatal excursion to West Point. In Sargent's, "Life of Andre," we find a very interesting

description of this mansion, and of the scenes witnessed there in olden time.

"Where now in New York is the unalluring and
crowded neighborhood of Second avenue and Thirty-fifth street, stood, in 1780, the ancient Bowerie or
country seat of Jacobus Kip. Built in 1655, of
bricks brought from Holland, encompassed by pleasant trees and in easy view of the sparkling waters
of Kip's Bay, on the East river, the mansion remained, even to our own times, in the possession of one
of its founder's line.

"When Washington was in the neighborhood,
Kip's house had been his quarters. When Howe
crossed from Long Island on Sunday, September
15th, 1776, he debarked at the rocky point hard by,
and his skirmishers drove our people from their position behind the dwelling. Since then it had
known many guests. Howe, Clinton, Kniphausen,
Percy were sheltered by its roof. The aged owner,
with his wife and daughter, remained. But they
had always an officer of distinction quartered with
them. And if a part of the family were in arms for
Congress, as is alleged, it is certain that others were
active for the Crown.

"Samuel Kip, of Kipsburg, led a cavalry troop
of his own tenantry, with great gallantry, in De Lancey's regiment. And despite severe wounds, sur-

vived long after the war, a heavy pecuniary sufferer by the cause which, with most of the landed gentry of New York, he had espoused.

"In 1780, it was held by Colonel Williams, of the 80th royal regiment. And here, on the evening of the 19th of September, he gave a dinner to Sir Henry Clinton and his staff, as a parting compliment to Andre. The aged owner of the house was present; and when the Revolution was over he described the scene and the incidents of that dinner. At the table Sir Henry Clinton announced the departure of Andre next morning, on a secret and most important expedition, and added, 'Plain John Andre will come back Sir John Andre.'

"How brilliant soever the company," Mr. Sargent adds, "how cheerful the repast, its memory must ever have been fraught with sadness to both host and guests. It was the last occasion of Andre's meeting his comrades in life. Four short days gone, the hands, then clasped by friendship, were fettered by hostile bonds. Yet nine days more and the darling of the army, the youthful hero of the hour, had dangled from a gibbet."

For two hundred and twelve years this mansion of venerable memories remained. Then it was swept away by the resistless tide of an advancing population. The thronged pavements of Thirty-fifth street now pass over the spot, where two centuries ago the most illustrious men crowded the banqueting hall, and where youth and beauty met in the dance and song. In view of these ravages of time, well may we exclaim in the impressive words óf Burke, "What shadows we are and what shadows we pursue."

In the year 1774, John Adams rode from Boston to Philadelphia on horseback, to attend the first meeting of Congress. His journal contains an interesting account of this long and fatiguing tour. Coming from the puritanic simplicity of Boston, he was evidently deeply impressed with the style and splendor which met his eye in New York. In glowing terms he alludes to the elegance of their mode of living, to the architectural grandeur of their country seats; to the splendor of Broadway, and to the magnificent new church they were building, which was to cost one hundred thousand dollars.

The aristocratic families of New York were generally in favor of the Crown. They were not disposed to pay any special attention to a delegate to the democratic Congress. He had therefore no opportunity of witnessing the splendor of these ancient families. Two lawyers who had become wealthy by their professional labors, received him with honor. At their breakfast tables he beheld display, common enough in almost every genteel household at the present day, but to which he was quite unaccustomed in his frugal home at Quincy. One cannot but be amused in reading the following description of one of his entertainments :

"A more elegant breakfast I never saw; rich plate ; a very large silver coffee pot; a very large silver tea pot; napkins of the very finest materials; toast and bread and butter in great perfection. After breakfast a plate of beautiful peaches, another of pears and a muskmelon were placed on the table."

The Revolution proved the utter ruin of these great landed proprietors, who naturally espoused the cause of the British court. The habits of life to which they and their fathers had been accustomed necessarily rendered all the levelling doctrines of the Revolution offensive to them. They rallied around the royal banners and went down with them.

Some few of the landed proprietors espoused the cause of the people. Among others may be mentioned the Livingstons and the Schuylers, the Jays, the Laurences, and a portion of the Van Courtlands, and of the Morris family. Fortunately for the Patroon Van Rensselaer, he was a minor, and thus escaped the peril of attaching himself to either party.

Negro slavery in a mild form prevailed in these early years in New York. The cruel and accursed system had been early introduced into the colony. Most of the slaves were domestic servants, very few being employed in the fields. They were treated with personal kindness. Still they were bondmen, deprived of liberty, of fair wages, and of any chance of rising in the world. Such men cannot, by any possibility, be contented with their lot. Mr. William L. Stone, in his very interesting History of New York, writes:

"As far back as 1628, slaves constituted a portion of the population of New Amsterdam; and to such an extent had the traffic in them reached that, in 1709, a slave market was erected at the foot of Wall street, where all negroes who were to be hired or sold, stood in readiness for bidders. Their introduction into the colony was hastened by the colonial establishment of the Dutch in Brazil and upon the coast of Guinea, and also by the capture of Spanish and Portuguese prizes with Africans on board.

"Several outbreaks had already happened among the negroes of New Amsterdam; and the whites lived in constant anticipation of trouble and danger from them. Rumors of an intended insurrection, real or imaginary, would circulate, as in the negro

plot of 1712, and the whole city be thrown into a
state of alarm.   Whether there was any real danger
on these occasions, cannot now be known.   But the
result was always the same.   The slaves always suffered, many dying by the fagot or the gallows."

In the year 1741, a terrible panic agitated the
whole city in apprehension of an insurrection of the
slaves.   The most cruel laws had been passed to
hold them firmly in bondage.   The city then contained ten thousand inhabitants, two thousand of
whom were slaves.   If three of these, "black seed
of Cain," were found together, they were liable
to be punished by forty lashes on the bare back.
The same punishment was inflicted upon a slave
found walking with a club, outside of his master's
grounds without a permit.   Two justices could inflict any punishment, except amputation or death,
upon any slave who should make an assault upon
a Christian or a Jew.

A calaboose or jail for slaves stood on the Park
Common.   Many of the leading merchants in New
York were engaged in the slave trade.   Several fires
had taken place, which led to the suspicion that the
slaves had formed a plot to burn the city and massacre the inhabitants.   The panic was such that the
community seemed bereft of reason.   A poor, weak,
half-crazed servant-girl, Mary Burton, in a sailor's

boarding house, testified, after much importunity, that she had overheard some negroes conferring respecting setting the town on fire.

At first she confined her accusations to the blacks. Then she began to criminate white people, bringing charges against her landlord, his wife and other white persons in the household. In a History of this strange affair written at the time, by Daniel Horsmanden, one of the Justices of the Supreme Court, we read,

"The whole summer was spent in the prosecutions. A coincidence of slight circumstances was magnified, by the general terror, into violent presumptions. Tales collected without doors, mingling with the proofs given at the bar, poisoned the minds of the jurors, and this sanguinary spirit of the day suffered no check until Mary, the capital informer, bewildered by the frequent examinations and suggestions, began to touch characters which malice itself dare not suspect."

During this period of almost insane excitement, thirteen negroes were burned at the stake, eighteen were hanged, and seventy transported.

I cannot conclude this treatise upon the olden time better than by quoting the eloquent words of Mr. Kip:

"The dress, which had for generations been the

sign and symbol of a gentleman, gradually waned away, till society reached that charming state of equality in which it became impossible, by any outward costume, to distinguish masters from servants. John Jay says, in one of his letters, that with small clothes and buckles the high tone of society departed. In the writer's early day this system of the past was just going out. Wigs and powder and queues, breeches and buckles, still lingered among the older gentlemen, vestiges of an age which was vanishing away.

" But the high toned feeling of the last century was still in the ascendant, and had not yet succumbed to the worship of mammon, which characterizes this age. There was still in New York a reverence for the colonial families, and the prominent political men, like Duane, Clinton, Colden, Radcliff, Hoffman and Livingston, were generally gentlemen, both by birth and social standing. The time had not yet come when this was to be an objection to an individual in a political career. The leaders were men whose names were historical in the State, and they influenced society. The old families still formed an association among themselves, and intermarried, one generation after another. Society was therefore very restricted. The writer remembers in his childhood, when he went out with his father for his afternoon drive, he knew every carriage they met on the avenues.

"The gentlemen of that day knew each other well, for they had grown up together and their associations in the past were the same. Yet, what friendships for after-life did these associations form! There was, in those days, none of the show and glitter of modern times. But there was, with many of these families, particularly with those who had retained their landed estates and were still living in their old family homes, an elegance which has never been rivalled in other parts of the country. In his early days the writer has been much at the South; has staid at Mount Vernon when it was held by the Washingtons; with Lord Fairfax's family, at Ashgrove and Vancluse; but he has never elsewhere seen such elegance of living as was formerly exhibited by the old families of New York.

"One thing is certain, that there was a high tone prevailing at that time, which is now nowhere to be seen. The community then looked up to public men, with a degree of reverence which has never been felt by those who have succeeded them. They were the last of a race which does not now exist. With them died the stateliness of colonial times. Wealth came in and created a social distinction

16

which took the place of family; and thus society became vulgarized.

"The influences of the past are fast vanishing away, and our children will look only to the shadowy future. The very rule by which we estimate individuals has been entirely altered. The inquiry once was, 'Who is he?' Men now ask the question, 'How much is he worth?' Have we gained by the change?"

THE END.

Printed in the United States
25875LVS00002B/36

9 781417 948307